Victorious

God's Guidelines for Successful Living

Valy Vaduva
Author of *Grace Rediscovered*

Upper Room
Fellowship Ministry

Livonia, Michigan, USA

VICTORIOUS: *God's Guidelines for Successful Living*
© 2024 by Valy Vaduva

Published by Upper Room Fellowship Ministry (URFM)
Livonia, MI 48150
www.urfm.org

ISBN 978-1-930529-54-0 (sc)
ISBN 978-1-930529-57-1 (E-book)
Library of Congress Control Number: 2024910150

All rights reserved. No part of this book may be used or reproduced by any means, graphic, electronic, or mechanical, including photocopying, recording, taping, or by any information storage retrieval system without the author's written permission, except in the case of brief quotations embodied in critical articles and reviews.

This book is a work of non-fiction. Unless otherwise noted, the author and the publisher make no explicit guarantees as to the accuracy of the information contained in this book, and in some cases, the names of people and places have been altered to protect their privacy. The views expressed in this work are solely those of the author and do not necessarily reflect the opinions of the publisher.

Unless otherwise cited, scripture quotations are taken from the New American Standard Bible® (NASB), Copyright © 1960, 1962, 1963, 1968, 1971, 1972, 1973, 1975, 1977, 1995 by The Lockman Foundation. Used by permission.

Scripture quotations marked (CEV) are from the Contemporary English Version Copyright © 1991, 1992, 1995 by American Bible Society. Used by Permission.
The Good News Translation (2nd ed). 1992. New York: American Bible Society.
Scripture is taken from GOD'S WORD®, © 1995 God's Word to the Nations. Used by permission of Baker Publishing Group.

Because of the dynamic nature of the Internet, any web addresses or links contained in this book may have changed since publication and may no longer be valid. Cover design by Georgian Radulescu.

Dedication

I dedicate this book to all believers interested in walking victoriously as disciples of Christ's.

Contents

	Preface	i
1	The Greatest Needs of Humanity:	1
	1) *The Sins Problem*	
	2) *The Slavery to Sin Problem*	
2	God's Guidelines for Successful Living:	15
	1) *Spiritual Comprehension*	
	2) *Spiritual Calculation*	
	3) *Spiritual Submission*	
	4) *Spiritual Guidance*	
3	The Law of the Spirit of Life in Christ	42
4	The Law Empowers Sin	54
5	Lectio Divina: *Practicing God's Presence*	63
	Addendum A—*Supremacy of Christ*	73
	Addendum B—*Christ Plus Nothing*	86
	Addendum C—*Hidden with Christ in God*	94
	Upper Room Fellowship Ministry	107
	About the author	108

Preface

But when He, the Spirit of truth, comes, He will guide you into all the truth; for He will not speak on His own initiative, but whatever He hears, He will speak; and He will disclose to you what is to come. He will glorify Me, for He will take of Mine and will disclose it to you.
— John 16:13-14

Over the years of pastoral counseling and discipleship ministry, I have noticed that many believers feel defeated. They stumble repeatedly in the same areas of their lives. Even in my life, I have noticed that some aspects are difficult to overcome.

Recently, the Holy Spirit impressed upon my heart to prepare a series of studies about *"God's Guidelines for Successful Living."*[1] This book is based on the findings I preached in 2023 and early 2024. Some aspects of the book are inspired by Watchman Nee's book *The Normal*

---

[1] Autor's Note: The original title for my Bible Study series was *"God's Blueprint for Victorious Living."* But I sensed that the Holy Spirit wanted me to change the title to *"Victorious"* and the subtitle to *"God's Guidelines for Successful Living."*

Christian Life, which I quoted several times.

In this book, I zoomed into several critical spiritual aspects, such as *comprehension, calculation, submission,* and *guidance.* Some chapters are short, and some are longer, but all contain powerful spiritual truths. The book's last chapter introduces you to a powerful spiritual discipline— *Lectio Divina,* used by many believers today to deepen their intimacy with the Lord. At the end of the book, I offer my readers additional insightful information, primarily based on the Book of Colossians. I hope you will also read the addendums.

Now, I want to highlight a fundamental spiritual principle: *Believers are where they are today because of a series of decisions (or lack thereof) they made during their Christian life.* My wife and I are currently ministering to the local community by offering people Professional Christian Counseling (Elena), Spiritual Life Coaching, Discipleship, and Pastoral Counseling (Valy) from our private practice called *New Life Direction Counseling*[2], which we opened in 2018. Since then, we have ministered to many people who need assistance during their life challenges.

By God's grace, we continue to offer these services and enjoy seeing many lives restored and strengthened. However, this would not have been possible if we had ignored God's guidance in 2006. Thank God we listened to His voice!

Let me share a story from my life to help you understand this principle. This is not to show off or brag about where I am—*may it never be!* I'm still a disciple under construction and have not arrived yet (see Philippians 3:12–16).

---

[2] To learn more about our private practice, I invite you to visit https://newlifedirectioncounseling.com/.

Victorious

The Back Story of New Life Directions Counseling

In 2006, my wife and I flew back from the "Life in Christ" conference in Atlanta, Georgia. The speakers, the messages, and the fellowship were excellent. While on the plane, we concomitantly felt the Holy Spirit whispering something significant in our hearts. I guess when you are 33,000 ft. in the air, you feel closer to God.

I turned to my wife and said, *"God told me something. Do you want to know what the Holy Spirit impressed upon my heart?"* My wife said, *"I also sensed God telling me something important. But you go first."*

I told her: *"Guess what? God wants me to go back to school to get my master's degree in Spiritual Formation. Unbelievable, isn't it?"*

Then my wife told me: *"Wow! God also wants me to attend school for my master's degree in Christian Counseling. Hard to believe, right?"*

You must understand that our four children were in college or about to enroll in graduate studies. What God asked us to do didn't make sense whatsoever. However, early in our walk with the Lord, we learned to obey the voice of the Spirit even when His requests did not make any sense.

When we got home, we shared with our children what the Holy Spirit whispered to our hearts. They sided with God and told us to go ahead and follow His lead.

We prayed, talked to people, and looked for universities that offer these programs. It took us a while, but one thing led to another, and finally, we discovered that Spring Arbor University (a Christian institution not too far from where we live) offers master's degrees in Christian Counseling, Spiritual Formation, and

Leadership.

Since we did not have money to pay for these programs, in 2007, we filled out FAFSA forms to get student loans. While doing that, I remember telling my youngest daughter: *"Cristina, I am so sorry, but I will not be able to pay for your tuition at the University of Michigan!"* What she said was so sweet! *"Dad, it is better for you to listen to what the Holy Spirit wants you to do. One way or the other, God will provide for me too."* And, beyond our comprehension, He did.

Then 2008 came. Do you remember that year? Of course, you do; everybody remembers it—it was the year of the housing market collapse. According to the Federal Reserve History, the financial crisis was so deep that it was labeled "the Great Recession."[1] Moreover, according to Investopedia: "This period ranks among the most devastating in U.S. financial market history."[2]

Banks were collapsing left and right. In addition, the credit and subprime mortgage crisis and government bailout led to the enormous financial disaster in September 2008.[3]

My family was also greatly affected by that turmoil. I will never forget the emotional stress I endured during that period. Just imagine for a second what might have happened if God had told us in 2008 what He told us in 2006. We would probably have responded: *"Thank You, God, but no, thank You! Don't You see the financial mess we are in?"* But, since we said *"yes"* two years ago, we did not back down from following God's plan.

The student loans arrived just before my 49th birthday, and we started our programs. One credit after another, one course after another, one white paper, and project after another led to our graduation. In 2011, we completed the master's programs and were ready to go in a completely new direction. Praise God! *And the rest is history.*

I hope you see that God is the main reason we have our private practice and the stewardship of ministering to people in need. To God be the glory!

Therefore, I fervently pray that my readers will gain a deeper understanding of how God intends His children to live successful and fulfilling Christian lives. I also hope my readers will be willing to apply the guidelines and principles highlighted in this book, leading to triumph over sin and flesh.

Before you start reading, pause and pray that the Holy Spirit will give you a deeper understanding of the theological truths throughout the chapters of this book. The following prayer is adapted after Ephesians 1:15-22:

> *Father God, please give me a spirit of wisdom and revelation so that I can understand the teachings of Scripture. Open the eyes of my heart so I can know Jesus more profoundly and realize who I am in Him.*
>
> *Father, I desire to consistently experience victory over sin and flesh. I know with my intellect that You raised Christ from the dead through the Holy Spirit with mighty power, and with Him, You raised me, too. But I also need Your help to experience this truth with my heart. I also know with my head that I'm seated with Jesus in the heavenly places, but I have difficulties comprehending this reality with my heart.*
>
> *O, God, You know my specific struggles and desire not to sin, but the more I try, the more defeated I feel. There must be a way for me to overcome my fleshly desires. Please make your principles and guidelines for*

victorious living plain to me! In Your Son's name, I pray, amen, and amen.

I have also been praying for you, so I expect the Holy Spirit to highlight the spiritual guidelines you must incorporate by faith into your life.

May God bless you, my beloved!

Valy Vaduva

Pastor / Teacher

---

[1] "The Great Recession and Its Aftermath," www.federalreservehistory.org. Accessed on April 15, 2024.
https://www.federalreservehistory.org/essays/great-recession-and-its-aftermath.

[2] Paul Kosakowski, "The Fall of the Market in the Fall of 2008" updated June 30, 2023. www.investopedia.com. Accessed on April 15, 2024.
https://www.investopedia.com/articles/economics/09/subprime-market-2008.asp.

[3] For more details regarding the Freddie Mac and Fannie Mae bailout and the Lehman Brothers bankruptcy that triggered the global recession, feel free to check out "A Reminder of the Corruption That Helped Birth the Biggest Bailout in History," published on July 18, 2013, on www.house.gov. Accessed on April 17, 2024. https://bit.ly/4d1eFob. Or visit www.thebalancemoney.com.
By the way, the bailout cost American taxpayers nearly $200 billion. Not fair, right?

-1-

The Greatest Needs of Humanity

They have all turned aside, together they have become corrupt; There is no one who does good, not even one.
— Psalm 14:3

Wretched man that I am! Who will set me free from the body of this death?
— Romans 7:24

Every human born into this world is spiritually dead (Ephesians 2:1–3), a slave to sin (John 8:34), and belongs to the devil (John 8:44). Generally speaking, the problem of humanity is dual in nature.

On the one hand, there are the **transgressions**—the sum total of the sins committed by the entire world. All human beings, according to Romans 3:23, *"have sinned and* *fall short of the glory of God."* And David writes: *"There is no one who does good, not even one"* (Psalm 14:3b). At a personal level, because I have committed all sorts of sins, I need forgiveness for what I have done.

On the other hand, is **sinfulness**—I am a sinner, a slave to the power of sin (or the sin principle). Because of my condition, I desperately need complete deliverance from what I am. Paul writes: *"Wretched man that I am! Who will set me free from the body of this death?"* (Romans 7:24).

Therefore, as spiritually dead, unregenerated slaves to sin and under Satan's authority, human beings need *redemption* and *deliverance.*

A. Redemption—*forgiveness of sins*

God's solution for redemption and forgiveness for sins is *Christ's death.* Jesus died for your forgiveness.

Paul writes:

> For He rescued us from the domain of darkness and transferred us to the kingdom of His beloved Son, in whom we have redemption, the forgiveness of sins. (Colossians 1:13–14)

B. Deliverance from sin

As regenerated, born-again, saved believers, we need **deliverance** from **sin**. God's solution for our need for deliverance from sin is *the resurrected life of Jesus.*

Paul writes:

> But God, being rich in mercy, because of His great love with which He loved us, even when we were

dead in our transgressions, made us alive together with Christ (by grace you have been saved), and raised us up with Him, and seated us with Him in the heavenly places in Christ Jesus. (Ephesians 2:4–6)

Furthermore, if we look carefully at Paul's teaching in the book of Romans, we observe two aspects of Christ's redeeming work for us. These two theological concepts are captured best by Paul in Romans 5:10: *"For if while we were enemies we were* **reconciled** *to God through the* **death of His Son**, *much more, having been reconciled, we shall be* **saved** *by* **His life**.*"* One concept is *His death for reconciliation*, and the second is *His life for salvation*.

As I already stated, since my problem is dual in nature: "I need forgiveness for what I have done (*my sinfulness*), but I also need deliverance from what I am (*a sinner, slave to sin*)."[4]

Interestingly, Paul writes primarily about **sins** in his letter to Romans 1:1 to Romans 5:11. Then, from Romans 5:12 to Romans 8;39, Paul writes primarily about the **sin principle**. The point is that we need both forgiveness from all our transgressions and deliverance from our slavery to sin.

Reflection Questions:

Please reflect upon the following questions, briefly elaborate, then share your thoughts with a friend or with your small group.

1. What did the Holy Spirit whisper to your heart through this chapter?

_____
_____

2. What new concepts did you learn from this chapter? Which idea are you committed to implementing in your life?

_____
_____

3. *"If bondage to sin comes by birth, then deliverance from sin comes by death."* What do you think about this statement?

_____
_____
_____

4. *"The Cross is thus the power of God which translates us from Adam to Christ."* What do you think about this statement?

_____
_____
_____

5. Please list the best aha moments you had while reading this chapter.

_____
_____

Victorious

Endnotes:

[4] Watchman Nee, *The Normal Christian Life*, (Tyndale House Publishers, Wheaton, IL, 1977), 14.

I. The Sin Problem

For all have sinned and fall short of the glory of God,
— Romans 3:23

For the wages of sin is death, but the free gift of God is eternal life in Christ Jesus our Lord.
— Romans 6:23

Kind David writes: "Behold, I was brought forth in iniquity, and in sin, my mother conceived me" (Psalm 51:5). All human beings are born into this world as sinners, therefore, spiritually separated from God. God took care of the sin problem, once and for all, by the Blood of the Lamb.

Peter writes:

> Knowing that you were not redeemed with perishable things like silver or gold from your futile way of life inherited from your forefathers, but with <u>precious blood, as of a lamb</u> unblemished and spotless, the **blood of Christ**. (1 Peter 1:18–19)

Nee brings an interesting view of the Blood of Christ. He writes: "In the Scriptures, the Blood of Christ is shown to operate effectually in these three ways:

- God-ward (*for our forgiveness*),
- Man-ward (*for our conscience*),
- Satan-ward (*for Satan accusations*)."[5]

A. *Because of Christ's Blood, God's children are considered saints.*

The author of Hebrews writes: "Therefore, Jesus also, that He might sanctify the people through His own blood, suffered outside the gate" (Hebrews 13:12).

B. *Through the Blood of Christ, God's children, overcame Satan's accusations.*

According to the Bible: "And they overcame him because of the blood of the Lamb and because of the word of their testimony, and they did not love their life even when faced with death" (Revelation 12:11).

C. *By the Blood of Christ, we can have a clear conscience.*

The Word of God states: "How much more will the blood of Christ, who through the eternal Spirit offered Himself without blemish to God, cleanse your conscience from dead works to serve the living God?" (Hebrews 9:14). I like Nee's conclusion: "The Blood of Christ wholly satisfies God."[6]

As is written in the Pentateuch: *"The blood shall be a sign for you on the houses where you live; and when I see the blood, I will pass over you, and no plague will befall you to destroy you when I strike the land of Egypt"* (Exodus 12:13).
If the blood of the natural lambs was enough to save the Israelites, the precious Blood of the Lamb of God (John 1:29b, Revelation 7:14, 12:11) is more than sufficient to save us.

Reflection Questions:

Please reflect upon the following questions, briefly elaborate, then share your thoughts with a friend or with your small group.

1. What did the Holy Spirit whisper to your heart through this chapter?

_____

_____

2. What new concepts did you learn from this chapter? Which idea are you committed to implementing in your life?

_____

_____

3. What are your thoughts about the concept that the Blood of Jesus, operates effectually in three ways.

_____

_____

_____

4. Do you believe the blood is more than sufficient to save us (past, present, and future)? Please explain.

_____

_____

_____

5. Please list the best aha moments you had while reading this chapter.

_____

_____

Endnotes:

[5] *The Normal Christian Life*, 16.
[6] Nee, 19.

II. The Slavery to Sin Problem

Jesus answered them, "Truly, truly, I say to you, everyone who commits sin is the slave of sin. The slave does not remain in the house forever; the son does remain forever. So if the Son makes you free, you will be free indeed."
— John 8:34–36

In His foreknowledge, God envisioned that through the sacrifice of His only Begotten Son on the Calvary cross, the Father would resolve the problem of our *transgressions* and our *bondage to sin*.

It is imperative to understand the whole meaning of the cross. In his book *The Normal Christian Life*, Watchman New uses the term *"cross"* as "the entire redemptive work accomplished historically in the death, burial, resurrection, and ascension of the Lord Jesus Himself (Philippians 2:8, 9), and in a wider sense, the union of believers with Him therein through grace (Romans 6:4; Ephesians 2:5, 6)."[7]

In his letters, Paul explains that the Blood of Christ is the result of the work of the cross. He states: "and through Him to reconcile all things to Himself, having made peace **through the blood of His cross**" (Colossians 1:20a).

In my book *Fullness of Christ*, I wrote:

> The cross is the single point in the universe where, in God's spiritual economy, we are identified with

Christ in all the facets of His work.[8]

In other words, we are united with Christ through His death, burial, resurrection, and ascension. It is vitally important to have a comprehensive understanding of the complete work of Christ accomplished once and for all on the cross of Calvary. We must incorporate both aspects of the cross: Christ's death (*blood*) and His resurrection (*zoe life*).

It is worth repeating that **the blood deals with our sins**—*offering us forgiveness of sins*, and **the cross deals with the sinner**—*providing us deliverance from the body of sin (our old man)*. We are sinners because we are born out of Adam. After regeneration, we are declared saints. In other words, because we are no longer in Adam but in Christ, we are not sinners but saints. Nee writes: "The blood procures our pardon for what we have done; the Cross procures our deliverance from what we are."[9] Reflect on this statement. *If bondage to sin comes by birth, then deliverance from sin comes by death.* Therefore: "Death is the secret of emancipation."[10] (See also Romans 6:2.)

Based on Pauline theology (the teaching in the letters written by the apostle Paul, Christ died as our representative. His death and His resurrection are inclusive. Paul calls Christ the **last Adam**. "So also, it is written, "The first MAN, Adam, BECAME A LIVING SOUL." The **last Adam** became a life-giving spirit" (1 Corinthians 15:45).

I like the way Watchman Nee explains this:

> As the last Adam, Christ is the sum-total of humanity and as the second Man, He is the Head of a new race. So, we have here **two unions**, <u>the</u>

<u>one relating to His death</u> and <u>the other to His resurrection</u>. In the first place, His union with the (human) race as "the last Adam" began historically at Bethlehem and ended at the cross and the tomb. In it He gathered up into Himself all that was in Adam and took it to judgment and death.

In the second place, our union with Him as "the second Man" begins in resurrection and ends in eternity—which is to say, it never ends—for having in His death done away with the first man in whom God's purpose was frustrated, He rose again as Head of a new race of men, in whom that purpose shall be fully realized.[11]

What can I say? Only God, in His infinite wisdom, could come up with something like this! Our Father used the cross to accomplish all of this. I wholeheartedly side with the Psalmist: "Oh give thanks to the LORD, for He is good, for His lovingkindness is everlasting" (Psalm 107:1).

No wonder Paul writes so confidently about the cross: "For the word of the cross is foolishness to those who are perishing, but to us who are being saved it is the power of God" (1 Corinthians 1:18).

Nee writes: "We died in Him as the last Adam; We live in Him as the second Man. **The Cross is thus the power of God which translates us from Adam to Christ.**"[12]

I firmly believe that without full knowledge, by revelation, of the truth explained briefly above, it is impossible to have deliverance from sin, the world, and the devil.

Reflection Questions:

Please reflect upon the following questions, briefly elaborate, then share your thoughts with a friend or with your small group.

1. What did the Holy Spirit whisper to your heart through this chapter?

_____
_____

2. What new concepts did you learn from this chapter? Which idea are you committed to implementing in your life?

_____
_____

3. Does it make sense that *redemption from our sins* and *deliverance from our sinfulness* are part of our salvation?

_____
_____

4. Does it make sense that we need *Christ's death* for **reconciliation**, and *Christ's resurrected life* for **salvation** (progressive sanctification?

_____
_____

5. Please list the best aha moments you had while reading this chapter.

_____
_____

Endnotes:

[7] Nee, *The Normal Christian Life*, 31, 32.
[8] Valy Vaduva, *Fullness of Christ* (Upper Room Fellowship Ministry, Livonia, MI, 2018), 13.
[9] Nee, 36.
[10] Ibid, 42.
[11] Ibid, 46.
[12] Ibid, 47.

-2-

God's Guidelines for Successful Living

But thanks be to God, who always leads us in triumph in Christ, and manifests through us the sweet aroma of the knowledge of Him in every place.
— 2 Corinthians 2:14

Many of you might exclaim: *"Oh, my goodness! Is there a blueprint for complete victory?"* I'm happy to tell you that there is. The book of Romans offers such a plan.

Before presenting the plan, let me provide a simple outline of the first eight chapters of this important letter.

1. Sins and sinfulness

This is the theme covered by Paul in chapters 1:18 through 3:20.

2. Salvation

The theology of salvation is explained in chapters 3:21 through 5:11.[3]

3. Sanctification

This topic is taught in chapters 5:12 through 6:23.

4. Struggle

Paul explains in Romans 7 the frustration that all believers, without exception, identify with. Paul is saying this agony comes from realizing that the flesh cannot fulfill the requirements of God's Law.

5. Spiritual Victory

The pathway to living a victorious Christian life is the theme Paul addresses in Chapters 8:1–27.

6. Security

As born-again, Spirit-filled believers, we have 100% security in Christ by God's grace. The apostle Paul discusses this vital aspect in Romans 8:28–39.

Going over all six sections will require a lot of space and will take a long time. In this book, I am going to cover parts of number *3, Sanctification,* (Paul teaches about

---

[3] For those of you who would like to explore the topic of sin, sinfulness, and salvation in-depth, I recommend reading at least chapter 1, "The Extraordinary Gift," from my book *The Journey of Transformation*. Click on the link to get the book: https://bit.ly/41HPFfp.

sanctification in Romans chapters 5:12 through 6:23), and parts of number 5, *Spiritual Victory* (the pathway to living a victorious Christian life is discussed by Paul in Romans chapters 8:1–27).

The most important aspect to remember is that *through the cross/death of Christ, we kissed goodbye to our old history, and through the resurrection of Jesus, we welcome in the new life.* Our death with Christ is a historical fact. Paul clearly states: "Christ died for us" (Romans 5:8b). And *"We have died with Christ"* (Romans 6:8a). According to Watchman Nee: *"This [is] the Gospel for Christians."*[13]

Furthermore, Nee writes:

> Our crucifixion can never be made effective by will or by effort, but only by accepting what the Lord Jesus did on the Cross. Our eyes must be opened to see the finished work of Calvary.[14]

Now, I invite you to pause for a few minutes and read Romans 6:1–14 slowly and meditatively. Let us briefly analyze the main points of this chapter.

After carefully studying Romans 6:1–23 and Romans 8:1–27, fourfold realities are emerging:

- *Spiritual Comprehension*
- *Spiritual Calculation*
- *Spiritual Submission*
- *Spiritual Guidance*

In the following pages, we will briefly discuss these spiritual principles.

Reflection Questions:

Please reflect upon the following questions, briefly elaborate, then share your thoughts with a friend or with your small group.

1. What did the Holy Spirit whisper to your heart through this chapter?

_____
_____

2. What new concepts did you learn from this chapter? Which idea are you committed to implementing in your life?

_____
_____

3. What do you think about *God's Guidelines for Successful Living?*

_____
_____
_____
_____

4. What is the "Gospel for Christians"? What do you think about the "Gospel for Christians"?

_____
_____
_____
_____

5. Please list the best aha moments you had while reading this chapter.

_____
_____

Victorious

Endnotes:

[13] Watchman Nee, 52.
[14] Ibid, 52.

I. Spiritual Comprehension

Or do you not know that all of us who have been baptized into Christ Jesus have been baptized into His death?
— Romans 6:3

Before unwrapping this step, let me briefly overview Romans 6:1–5. Feel free to read the endnotes to see the original Greek words used by Paul and better understand their meaning.

> What shall we say then? Are we to continue in *sin*[15] so that *grace*[16] may increase? May it never be! How shall we *who died*[17] to sin still, **live** in it?[18] Or do you not *know*[19] that all of us who have been *baptized*[20] into Christ Jesus have been baptized into His death? Therefore, we have been *buried*[21] with Him through baptism into death, so that as Christ was raised from the dead through the glory of the Father, so we too might *walk*[22] in newness of life. For if we have become *united with Him*[23] in the *likeness*[24] of His death, certainly, we shall certainly be in the likeness of His resurrection.

Paul asks a series of rhetorical questions and provides accurate answers. *Should we continue sinning?* Of course not. (v. 1 and 2). The way Paul poses the question in verse 3 *"Or do you not know…?"* It sounds like the apostle is wondering whether believers really understand this fundamental truth for sure. His main argument in these few verses is that *we have been baptized into His death.* (v. 3).

Let me ask you: *When was Christ buried?* Of course, we all know that Jesus died on a Roman Cross on Good Friday under Pontius Pilate. *When was Christ raised from the dead?* The Holy Spirit raised the Lord Jesus from the dead "on the third day according to the Scriptures" (1 Corinthians 15:4b), on the one and only Resurrection Sunday, most likely in 33 AD.

Romans 6:5 states the following important argument: "For if we have become united with Him in the *likeness of His death*, certainly we shall also be in *the likeness of His resurrection.*" Please review again what *"likeness"* means in Greek. Please observe that both *His death* and *His resurrection* are part of what happens to us, too. Wow! Mind-boggling. Let us continue with verses 6 to 8.

Paul writes:

> *Knowing* [25]this, that our *old self*[26] was *crucified*[27] with Him, in order that our body of sin might be *done away with,*[28] so that we would no longer be *slaves*[29] to sin; for he who has died is freed from sin. *Now if we have died with Christ, we believe that we shall also live with Him.* (Romans 6:6–8)

In other words, by incorporating the Greek meaning of the words in bold, Paul is saying:

> We came to **know** (*spiritual comprehension of this spiritual reality*) that our **old man** (*what we used to be in Adam*) was already **crucified** together with Christ, so that our **body of sin** (*the sin-factory in us,* the way Nee calls it in *The Normal Christina*

Life) was rendered inoperative, so we would no longer be **slaves** to sin (*having no other choice but serve sin and be devoted to it*). *Death with Christ means freedom from sin.* Since our death is a historical fact (*we also died with Christ in 33 AD*), we firmly believe that this fact empowers us to enjoy Christ's resurrected (zoe) life.

I want to make sure that this spiritual reality is crystal clear—*because we are in Christ, we are dead to sin.* However, be on the alert! **Sin is not dead.** If we give sin an opportunity, we can very easily sin. I want to emphasize that if a believer sins, it is not because they are still a slave to sin. No, no, and no! They sin because Satan and the world deceived them, and, as a result, they listened to the flesh instead of the Spirit.

Reflection Questions:

Please reflect upon the following questions, briefly elaborate, then share your thoughts with a friend or with your small group.

1. What did the Holy Spirit whisper to your heart through this chapter?

_____

_____

2. What new concepts did you learn from this chapter? Which idea are you committed to implementing in your life?

_____

_____

3. Did you know before reading this chapter that *"you died with Christ almost 200 years ago"*?

_____

_____

_____

4. Did you know before that *"you are dead to sin"*?

_____

_____

_____

5. Please list the best aha moments you had while reading this chapter.

_____

_____

_____

Endnotes:

[15] Hamartia. Strong Greek # 266: ἁμαρτία, meaning: missing the mark; hence: (a) guilt, sin, (b) a fault, failure (in an ethical sense), sinful deed." www.biblehub.com. Accessed on April 18, 2023. https://biblehub.com/greek/266.htm.
[16] Charis. Strong Greek # 5485: χάρις, meaning: grace, kindness. www.biblehub.com. Accessed on April 18, 2023. https://biblehub.com/greek/5485.htm.
[17] Hotines and apothnéskó. Strong Greek # 3748 οἵτινες, meaning: whoever, anyone who) and # 599 ἀποθνῄσκω, meaning: I am dying, am about to die. www.biblehub.com. Accessed on April 18, 2023. https://biblehub.com/greek/599.htm.
[18] Zaó. Strong Greek # 2198, ζήσομεν, meaning: I live, am alive. www.biblehub.com. Accessed on April 18, 2023. https://biblehub.com/greek/2198.htm.
[19] Agnoeite. Strong Greek # 50, ἀγνοεῖτε, meaning: to be ignorant, not to know, sometimes with the idea of willful ignorance. www.biblehub.com. Accessed on April 18, 2023. https://biblehub.com/greek/50.htm.
[20] Baptizó. Strong Greek # 907, ἐβαπτίσθημεν, meaning: to dip, sink, submerge. www.biblehub.com. Accessed on April 18, 2023. https://biblehub.com/greek/907.htm.
[21] Sunthaptó. Strong Greek # 4916, συνθάπτω, meaning: to bury with, to bury along. www.biblehub.com. Accessed on April 18, 2023. https://biblehub.com/greek/4916.htm.
[22] Peripateó. Strong Greek # 4043, περιπατήσωμεν. Meaning: to walk, to conduct my life. www.biblehub.com. Accessed on April 18, 2023. https://biblehub.com/greek/4043.htm.
[23] Sumphutos. Strong Greek # 4854, σύμφυτοζōēs, ὁμοίωμα, ατος, meaning: congenital, hence united with meaning. www.biblehub.com. Accessed on April 18, 2023. https://biblehub.com/greek/4854.htm.
[24] Homoióma: Strong Greek # 3667: ὁμοιώματι, meaning: that which is made like (something). www.biblehub.com. Accessed on April 20, 2023.
[25] Ginóskó. Strong Greek # 1097 γινώσκω, and means: to come to know, recognize, perceive. www.biblehub.com. Accessed on April 18, 2023. https://biblehub.com/greek/1097.htm.
[26] Palaios. Strong Greek # 3820 παλαιός, ά, όν, and means: old, ancient. www.biblehub.com. Accessed on April 18, 2023. https://biblehub.com/greek/3820.htm.

Victorious

---

²⁷ Sustauroó. Strong Greek # 4957 συνεσταυρώθη, meaning: to crucify together with. www.biblehub.com. Accessed on April 18, 2023. https://biblehub.com/greek/4957.htm.

²⁸ Katargeó. Strong Greek # 2673, καταργέω, and means: to render inoperative, abolish. www.biblehub.com. Accessed on April 18, 2023. https://biblehub.com/greek/2673.htm.

²⁹ Douleuein. Strong Greek # 1398:, δουλεύειν, meaning: to be a slave, to serve, to be devoted. www.biblehub.com. Accessed on April 18, 2023. https://biblehub.com/greek/1398.htm.

II. Spiritual Calculation

Even so consider yourselves to be dead to sin, but alive to God in Christ Jesus. Therefore, do not let sin reign in your mortal body so that you obey its lusts,
— *Romans 6:11–12*

Before explaining this step, I would like to give Romans 6:9–10 context.
Paul writes:

> *Knowing*[30] that Christ, having been raised from the dead, is never to die again; death no longer is *master over*[31] Him. For the death that He died, He died to sin once for all; but the life that He lives, He lives to God.

The thought Paul underlines in verses 9 and 10 is this:

We are fully aware that Christ died once and for all, He was raised from the dead, and it is impossible for death to master over the Resurrected Lord. Christ lives forever and lives entirely to God.

Now we can understand better what *consider—spiritual calculation* really means.
Paul writes:

> Even so, *consider/count* [32] yourselves to be dead to sin, but alive to God in Christ Jesus. Therefore, do

not let sin *reign*[33] in your mortal body so that you *obey*[34]its *lusts*.[35] (Romans 6:11–12)

In other words, Paul is saying:

Go ahead. *Calculate things from the view of the cross,* **draw the most logical conclusion**, and *then decide accordingly*. Based on the facts, the bottom line is: "*Stop allowing sin to lord over your life. Don't listen for a second to any passionate longings and desires springing forth in your mortal body.*"

I also like the way Eugene Peterson renders Romans 6:6–11:

Could it be any clearer? *Our old way of life was nailed to the cross with Christ,* a decisive end to that sin-miserable life—no longer captive to sin's demands! What we believe is this: *If we get included in Christ's sin-conquering death, we also get included in his life-saving resurrection.* We know that when Jesus was raised from the dead, it was a signal of the end of death-as-the-end. Never again will death have the last word. *When Jesus died, He took sin down with Him, but alive, He brings God down to us.* From now on, think of it this way: *Sin speaks a dead language that means nothing to you;* God speaks your mother tongue, and you hang on every word. **You are dead to sin and alive to God.** That's what Jesus did.

Nicely said, isn't it? Thank You, God, for Your amazing provision for Your children!

Reflection Questions:

Please reflect upon the following questions, briefly elaborate, then share your thoughts with a friend or with your small group.

1. What did the Holy Spirit whisper to your heart through this chapter?

_____

_____

2. What new concepts did you learn from this chapter? Which idea are you committed to implementing in your life?

_____

_____

3. What do you think about the fact that *"your dead to sin"* but, unfortunately *"sin is not dead"*?

_____

_____

_____

_____

4. What are you supposed to *"calculate"*?

_____

_____

_____

5. Please list the best aha moments you had while reading this chapter.

_____

_____

Victorious

Endnotes:

[30] Eidotes. Strong Greek # 1492 εἰδότες, meaning: be aware, behold, consider, perceive. www.biblehub.com. Accessed on April 18, 2023. https://biblehub.com/greek/1492.htm.

[31] Kurieuei. Strong Greek # 2961 κυριεύει, meaning: to be lord of, rule over, have authority over. www.biblehub.com. Accessed on April 18, 2023. https://biblehub.com/greek/2961.htm.

[32] Logizomai. Strong Greek # 3049 λογίζεσθε, meaning: to reckon, to consider, to count, to decide, to conclude; to think. www.biblehub.com. Accessed on April 18, 2023. https://biblehub.com/greek/3049.htm. Moreover, logízomai, is the root of the English terms "logic, logical" and it means to compute, "take into account," and come to a "bottom-line," reason to a logical conclusion and decide accordingly.

[33] Basileuetō. Strong Greek # 936 βασιλευέτω, meaning: to be king, to lord/reign over. www.biblehub.com. Accessed on April 18, 2023. https://biblehub.com/greek/936.htm.

[34] Hupakouein. Strong Greek # 5219 ὑπακούειν, meaning: to listen, attend to, obey. www.biblehub.com. Accessed on April 18, 2023. https://biblehub.com/greek/5219.htm.

[35] Epithumiais. Strong Greek # 1939 ἐπιθυμίαις, meaning: desire, passionate longing, lust. www.biblehub.com. Accessed on April 18, 2023. https://biblehub.com/greek/1939.htm.

III. Spiritual Submission

Therefore, I urge you, brethren, by the mercies of God, to present your bodies a living and holy sacrifice, acceptable to God, which is your spiritual service of worship.
— Romans 12:1

After the things we discussed before, in Romans 6:13–14, Paul writes:

> And do not go on **presenting/yielding** [36]the members of your body to sin as **instruments** [37]of unrighteousness; but present yourselves to God as those alive from the dead, and your members as instruments of righteousness to God. For sin shall not be **master/rule over** [38]you, for you are not under **Law** [39]but under **grace**. [40]

In other words, after looking carefully at the meaning of the Greek words highlighted in bold, Paul is admonishing us:

> Stop using your members (*all faculties of the mind, emotions, will, and all members of the body*) as weapons of sin; to the contrary, yield your entire being (*all members and all faculties*) to God's disposal as weapons of righteousness. Get this: **Sin has no legal right to rule over you.** Why? Simply because you are not under the Old Testament

LAW, but you are under the jurisdiction of God's GRACE.

Juxtapose this with Peterson's rendering of Romans 6:12–14:

That means *you must not give sin a vote in the way you conduct your lives.* Don't give it the time of day. Don't even run little errands that are connected with that old way of life. *Throw yourselves wholeheartedly and full-time*—remember, you've been raised from the dead—*into God's way of doing things. Sin can't tell you how to live.* After all, you're not living under that old tyranny any longer. **You're living in the freedom of God.**

I like that!

Daily Prayer:

Father God, I come before You this morning, and I am surrendering on your altar: all my faculties of the mind, emotions, will, and all my members at Your disposal as weapons of righteousness.
I declare that sin does not have any legal right over me. Therefore, I am asking You to empower me to live according to my spiritual identity. I also declare that I am dead to sin and alive to You, Father. I pray, in the wonderful name of Jesus Christ. Amen.

Reflection Questions:

Please reflect upon the following questions, briefly elaborate, then share your thoughts with a friend or with your small group.

1. What did the Holy Spirit whisper to your heart through this chapter?
_____
_____

2. What new concepts did you learn from this chapter? Which idea are you committed to implementing in your life?
_____
_____

3. What do you think about the fact that *"you are dead to sin"* but, unfortunately *"sin is not dead"*?
_____
_____
_____

4. What are you supposed to *"calculate"*?
_____
_____
_____

5. Please list the best aha moments you had while reading this chapter.
_____
_____
_____

Victorious

Endnotes:

[36] Paristanete. Strong Greek # 3936 παριστάνετε, meaning: to place beside, to present. www.biblehub.com. Accessed on April 18, 2023. https://biblehub.com/greek/3936.htm.

[37] Hoopla. Strong Greek # 3696 ὅπλα, meaning: a tool or a weapon. www.biblehub.com. Accessed on April 18, 2023. https://biblehub.com/greek/3696.htm.

[38] Kurieusei. Strong Greek # 2961 κυριεύσει, meaning: to be lord of, to rule or have authority over. www.biblehub.com. Accessed on April 18, 2023. https://biblehub.com/greek/2961.htm.

[39] Nomon. Strong Greek # 3551 νόμον, meaning: of law in general, or the Mosaic law, the Pentateuch, or the Old Testament in general. www.biblehub.com. Accessed on April 18, 2023. https://biblehub.com/greek/3551.htm.

[40] Charis. Strong Greek # 5485 χάριν, meaning: grace, kindness. www.biblehub.com. Accessed on April 18, 2023. https://biblehub.com/greek/5485.htm.

IV. Spiritual Guidance

So then, brethren, we are under obligation, not to the flesh, to live according to the flesh.
— *Romans 8:12*

Walking in the Spirit is the pathway to spiritual progress, spiritual growth, and spiritual victory. Paul addresses this theme in Romans 8:1–27. To experience these is part of the spiritual birthright of every genuine child of God.

Before diving into the fourth step: *Walking in the Spirit*, let's consider several important aspects:

A. *In Adam* or *in Christ* (cf. Romans 5:12 to Romans 6:23).

These terms determine our **position**. We are either *in Adam* or *in Christ*.

B. *According to the flesh* or *according to the Spirit* (cf. Romans 7:1 to Romans 8:39).

These aspects determine our **condition**. We are walking *in the flesh* or *in the Spirit*.

The Flesh versus The Spirit

We must understand that *the flesh* is linked with Adam, and *the Spirit* is linked with Christ. Nee writes: "To live in *the flesh* is to do something "out from" myself as *in Adam* ... Now the same is true of what is *in Christ*."[41]

The problem for many of us as Christians is that even though we are *in Christ,* we walk after *the flesh*, which is contrary to our spiritual position—walking after *the flesh* is living in our own direction and strength. If we desire to have our **condition** match our **position**, we must learn to walk after the Spirit. Paul writes: "For those who are according to the flesh set their minds on the things of the flesh, but those who are according to the Spirit, the things of the Spirit" (Romans 8:5).

I like what Nee has to say in this area:

> If I would know in experience all that is in Christ, then I must learn to live in the Spirit. Living in the Spirit means that I trust the Holy Spirit to do in me what I cannot do myself. This life is completely different from the life I would naturally live of myself. Each time I am faced with a new demand from the Lord, I look to Him to do in me what He requires of me. It is not a case of trying but of trusting; not of struggling but of resting in Him. If I have a hasty temper, impure thoughts, a quick tongue or a critical spirit, I shall not set out with a determined effort to change myself, but, reckoning myself dead in Christ to these things, I shall look to the Spirit of God to produce in me the needed purity or humility or meekness. This is what it means to "stand still, and see the salvation of the Lord, which he will work for you" (Exodus 14:13).[42]

In Philippians 3:1–11 Paul talks about *what "true circumcision"* really is and what it means to *walk in the Spirit*. He writes: "For we are the true circumcision, who worship in the Spirit of God and glory in Christ Jesus and put no confidence *in the flesh*" (Philippians 3:3). I strongly recommend reading the entire passage very carefully.

Moreover, Paul states that: "*although I myself might have confidence even in the flesh*" (Philippians 3:4a), because knowing Christ is invaluable "*I have suffered the loss of all things and count them but rubbish that I may gain Christ*" (Philippians 3:8b). Wow! In other words, he says:

> Forget about having a seat in Sanhedrim (the Senate in Jerusalem) and being a well-recognized professor of the Old Testament. *It does not matter.* **I want Christ more.**

What is the practical application for us today? How can I drive home Paul's example? I think we can reason this way:

> Even though I qualify for church leadership or Christian ministry because I have higher education and graduated magna cum laude from the most famous Christian Seminary. Besides, I belong to a good Christian family, well connected and well respected. However, I desire to know Christ and "*the power of His resurrection,*" so, for this reason, I consider all my past achievements as rubbish. Therefore, I have decided to place no confidence in the flesh; instead, I want to walk in the Spirit.

Paul understood the most critical aspects of life and discovered the secret of spiritual victory. Therefore, we should pay attention to his teachings.

I like the way Nee explains living in and trusting the Holy Spirit:

> If we live in the Spirit, if we walk by faith in the risen Christ, we can truly *stand aside* while the Spirit gains new victories over the flesh every day … Our victory lies in hiding in Christ, and in counting in simple trust upon His Holy Spirit to overcome in us our fleshly lusts with His own new desires. The Cross has been given to procure salvation for us; the Spirit has been given to produce salvation in us. Christ risen and ascended is the basis of our salvation; Christ in our hearts by the Spirit is its power.[43]

Let's look carefully at verses from Romans 8:12–13:

> So then, brethren, we are under obligation, **not to the flesh,** to live according to the flesh—for if you are living according to the flesh, you must die; but if by the Spirit you are putting to death the deeds of the body, you will live.

These verses accurately describe how to have victory over the flesh.

I encourage you to pay attention to what Paul says in Galatians 5:16: "But I say, walk by the Spirit, and **you will not carry out the desire of the flesh.**" The focus is on *walking by the Spirit,* not trying harder not to obey the flesh. As a result of this kind of walk, *you will not carry out the desire of the flesh.* **The distinction is extremely important.** Even in the Old Testament we have examples of God's grace.

Moses writes:

> Do not fear! Stand by and see the salvation of the LORD which He will accomplish for you today ... **The LORD will fight for you while you keep silent.** (Exodus 14:13–14)

Wow! Isn't this marvelous? I believe this passage has tremendous spiritual wisdom: *"The LORD will fight for you while you keep silent."* How hard could it be just to shut up? How difficult would it be to wait on the Lord? I guess, for whatever reason, for many of us, this isn't very easy! I think that Nee captured a fundamental concept regarding victory: *"Our victory lies in hiding in Christ, and in counting in simple trust upon His Holy Spirit to overcome in us our fleshly lusts with His own new desires."*[44]

Christ Is Our Life

Paul writes: "For you have died and your life is hidden with Christ in God" (Colossians 3:3). Dear beloved, it is vitally important to receive the revelation and the understanding that *"the life we live now is the life of Christ."* Paul received this revelation! In Galatians 2:20, he states: "I have been crucified with Christ; and it is no longer I who live, but Christ lives in me; and the life which I now live in the flesh I live by faith in the Son of God, who loved me and gave Himself up for me."

Many believers think the Christian life is just a changed life, but it is *an exchanged life*. Let us slowly read Paul's statement: *"and it is no longer I who live, but Christ lives in me."* **Christ Is Our Life!** For a complete teaching on the exchanged life, I highly encourage you to read, at least, the chapter called "The Greatest Exchange Ever,"[4] from *Fullness of Christ*.[45] I also appreciate that Nee brings to light a very interesting aspect of *regeneration* vs. *reproduction*.

He writes:

> Regeneration means that the life of Christ is planted in us by the Holy Spirit at our new birth. 'Reproduction' goes further: it means that new life grows and becomes manifest progressively in us, until the very likeness of Christ begins to be reproduced in our lives. That is what Paul means when he speaks of his travail for the Galatians "until Christ be formed in you" (Galatians 4:19).[46]

---

[4] For those of you who would like to explore the exchange life more, I highly recommend reading at least chapter 7 "The Greatest Exchange Ever," from my book *Fullness of Christ*. Click on the link to get the book: https://amzn.to/3mTcDBp.

Reflection Questions:

Please reflect upon the following questions, briefly elaborate, then share your thoughts with a friend or with your small group.

1. What did the Holy Spirit whisper to your heart through this chapter?
   _____
   _____

2. What new concepts did you learn from this chapter? Which idea are you committed to implementing in your life?
   _____
   _____

3. What do you think about the four concepts "*in Adam or in Christ*" and "*according to the flesh or according to the Spirit*"?
   _____
   _____
   _____
   _____

4. What are you supposed to "*have no confidence in the flesh*"?
   _____
   _____
   _____

5. Please list the best aha moments you had while reading this chapter.
   _____
   _____

Endnotes:

[41] *The Normal Christian Life*, 175.
[42] Nee, 176, 177.
[43] Ibid, 179, 180.
[44] Ibid, 179.
[45] *Fullness of Christ* (Upper Room Fellowship Ministry, Livonia, MI, 2018).
[46] Ibid, 180.

-3-

The Law of the Spirit of Life in Christ

For the law of the Spirit of life in Christ Jesus has set you free from the law of sin and of death.
— Romans 8:2

Isaac Newton, the great scientist (physicist and mathematician), was born in 1642 in Woolsthorpe, Lincolnshire, England. (Newton died in 1727 in London). He studied at Cambridge University in England.

Towards the end of the summer of 1666, he noticed an apple falling from the tree while meditating in the garden. At that moment, he wondered why the apple fell straight down rather than sideways or even upward. Starting from this incident, Isaac Newton developed the theory of gravity.[47]

> *"He showed that the force that makes the apple fall and that holds us on the ground is the same as the force that*

keeps the moon and planets in their orbits," said Martin Rees, a former president of Britain's Royal Society, the United Kingdom's national academy of science, which was once headed by Newton himself.

"His theory of gravity wouldn't have got us global positioning satellites," said Jeremy Gray, a mathematical historian at the Milton Keynes, U.K.-based Open University. *"But it was enough to develop space travel."*[48]

In 58 A.D., the Apostle Paul wrote the Epistle to the Romans. In chapter 7, Paul writes something unique. He realized that something in him (in his flesh) acts as a **law**—*principle*. Even if he wants to do good, he does not have the power to do it, and in the end, he acts precisely in opposition to what he had set his mind to accomplish. He writes: *"For I know that nothing good dwells in me, that is, in my flesh; for the willing is present in me, but the doing of the good is not"* (Romans 7:18).

Paul uses the word law. He writes:

> But I find this law in me: when I want to do good, evil sticks to me. Because, according to the inner man, I love the Law of God; but I see in my members another law, which fights against the law received by my mind, and holds me captive to the law of sin, which is in my members. (Romans 7:21–23).

Now, it is a good idea to recall the definition of the law:

A law is a universal principle that tells us that when the same conditions are met, the effect of this law is the same everywhere. A good example is the law of gravity. Wherever we go on the surface of this earth, the law of gravity is in effect. All objects are attracted to the center of the earth because of this law. It does not matter if it is a stone or a feather; they fall to the ground. Why? Because of gravitației.[49]

The law of gravity is the same in Rome, London, Bucharest, Tokyo, and New York.

The English engineer Sir George Cayley (b. 1773, in Scarborough, Yorkshire, d. 1854, in Brompton, Yorkshire) laid the foundations of aerodynamic science and is recognized as the inventor of the airplane. Cayley is called the world's first aeronautical engineer. He discovered the four aerodynamic forces of flight: 1. Lift (L), 2. Weight (Wt), 3. Thrust (T), 4. Drag (D).

The four laws of aerodynamics are:

1. *The first law of aerodynamics is the law of lift*

This law states that an object moving through a fluid (in this case, air) will experience a force perpendicular to the direction of motion. In the case of an airplane, this force is known as lift and is created by the shape of the wing. The curved shape of the wing, known as the airfoil, creates a difference in air pressure between the top and bottom surfaces of the wing, which results in a net upward force.

2. **The second law of aerodynamics is the law of weight**

   This law states that all objects have weight, which must be overcome for an object to achieve flight. In the case of an airplane, this weight includes the weight of the aircraft itself and its fuel, passengers, and cargo.

3. **The third law of aerodynamics is the law of thrust.**

   This law states that an airplane must have a forward force known as thrust to achieve and maintain flight. A jet engine or propeller typically provides this forward force, which propels the aircraft forward through the air.

4. **The fourth law of aerodynamics is the law of drag**

   This law states that all objects moving through a fluid will experience resistance, known as drag. In the case of an airplane, this drag is caused by the friction between the aircraft and the air around it. To overcome this drag, an airplane must be designed to be as streamlined as possible.[50]

The law of aerodynamics Lift force (L) overcomes the law of gravity Weight (W), therefore, people can fly in planes. The law of gravity is still in operation, but the law of aerodynamics is superior to it, which is why an aircraft can fly. For more details regarding this topic, I suggest reading at least chapter 6, "Sarx Blocks Spiritual Metamorphosis," from my book *The Journey of Transformation*.[5]

Chapter 7 of Romans ends with the apostle's agony and conclusion:

> Wretched man that I am! Who will set me free from the body of this death? Thanks be to God through Jesus Christ our Lord! So then, on the one hand I myself with my mind am serving the law of God, but on the other, with my flesh the law of sin. (Romans 7:24–25)

This agony is the inner struggle with which all believers identify, without exception. Practically speaking, this agony comes from the realization that the flesh cannot meet the demands of God's Law. So, what is the solution?

Chapter 8 of Romans explains Christ's solution for believers. Paul writes: Paul writes: "For the law of the Spirit of life in Christ Jesus has set you free from the law of sin and of death" (Romans 8:2). By incorporating what we have learned so far about the law of gravity and the law(s) of aerodynamics, we better understand how we can have complete victory in our Christian walk.

I am convinced that God fully knew that the Jewish people could not keep (conform to) the Law of the Old Testament. God's plan, from the eternity past, is to deliver us from the law of sin and of death (Romans 8:2b) by

---

[5] For those who would like to learn more about the flesh and the law of the Spirit, I suggest reading at least chapter 6, "Sarx Blocks Spiritual Metamorphosis," from my book *The Journey of Transformation*. Click on the link to get the book: https://bit.ly/41HPFfp.

introducing a new law, the law of the Spirit of life in Christ Jesus (Romans 8:2a).

I like the way Nee explains it:

> In just such a manner God delivers us from one law by introducing another law. The **law of sin and death** is there all the time, but God has put another law into operation—**the law of the Spirit of life in Christ Jesus**, and that law is strong enough to deliver us from the law of sin and death. You see, it is a law of life in Christ Jesus—the resurrection life that in Him has met death in all its forms and triumphed over it (Ephesians 1:19, 20).[51]

Clearly, we need to learn to operate by the superior law. The Christian life should not be based on self-effort. The Christian life should be the result of the *Law of the Spirit of life in Christ Jesus* operating inside us. Nee writes: "We don't need to force ourselves to speak our native language. In fact, we only have to exert willpower in order to do things we do not do naturally."[52] In other words, the secret of the victorious Christian life is not more effort (*in the flesh*) but more trust (*in the Spirit*) and resting more in God's arms. We have analyzed many verses already, but I think these verses from Philippians 2:12–13 are very powerful:

> So then, my beloved, just as you have always obeyed, not as in my presence only, but now much more in my absence, work out your salvation with fear and trembling; for it is God who is at work in you, both *to will* and *to work* for His good pleasure.

Do you see the secret here? **God is the One working inside us giving us the WILL to WORK according to His good pleasure.** I think Watchman Nee hits the nail on the head with this statement:

> We have spoken of trying and trusting and the difference between the two. Believe me, it is the difference between Heaven and hell. It is not something just to be talked over as a good thought; it is stark reality. *"Lord, I cannot do it; therefore, I will no longer try to do it."* This is the point where most of us fail. *"Lord, I cannot; therefore, I will take my hands off; from now on, I trust Thee for that."* I refuse to act; I depend on Him to act and then I enter fully and joyfully into the action He initiates. **It is not passivity; it is a most active life, trusting the Lord like that; drawing life from Him, taking Him to be our very life,** letting Him live His life in us as we go forth in His name.[53]

Once again, the **first aspect** *is living by faith in the Son of God* (Galatians 2:20b), and the **second aspect** *is walking by the Spirit* (Galatians 5:16a). Please note that Paul emphasizes: *"But if you are led by the Spirit, you are not under the Law"* (Galatians 5:18). Now, let's explore further what walking in the Spirit is all about.

I'm sure you have heard before that Romans chapter eight is probably the most powerful chapter in the New Testament or even in the entire Bible. We have already looked at Romans 8:2.

Let's continues:

For what the Law could not do, weak as it was

through the flesh, God did: sending His own Son in the likeness of sinful flesh and as an offering for sin, **He condemned sin in the flesh,** *so that the requirement of the Law might be fulfilled in us,* **who do not walk according to the flesh but according to the Spirit.** (Romans 8:3–4)

These verses are critically important for further understanding God's work in and through us. What is Paul saying? At least two main points:

1. God sent His own Son as an offering for sin *to forgive* us
2. God sent His Spirit *to transform* us

Now, through the power of the Spirit, God can fulfill His requirements according to His character expressed in the Law. What does it mean *to walk* according to the Spirit? Number one, this is *not work*; it is *a walk*. This distinction is crucial! If I think (and many times I do) that it is a work, I immediately stop operating under God's grace and fall under the Law's jurisdiction. But relying on my strength and abilities to please God is futile! It didn't work before, it does not work in the present, and it will not work in the future. Again, it is *not work*; it is *a walk*. **Since it is a walk, it means that I must be subject to the Spirit.**

Furthermore, Paul writes:

For those who *are according to the flesh* **set their minds on the things of the flesh** (Strong Greek # 4561: σάρξ, σαρκός, ἡ, **sarx,** meaning: of human origin or empowerment), but those *who are* *according to the Spirit*, **the things of the Spirit.** (Strong Greek # 4151: πνεῦμα, ατος, τό, **pneuma**: wind, spirit. See John 3:6-8). For **the mind set on the flesh is death, but the mind set on the Spirit is life and peace,** because the mind set on the flesh is hostile toward God; for it does not subject itself to the law of God, <u>for it is not even able to do so,</u> and **those who are in the flesh cannot please God.** (Romans 8:5–8)

Paul talks about two mindsets:

1. The *mindset of the flesh*
2. The *mindset of the Spirit*

According to Romans 8:5–8 the mindset we operate under makes a huge difference. Solomon explains: "For as he thinks in his heart, so is" (Proverbs 23:7a AMP). The mindset of the flesh results in death; implicitly, all the "performances" done under this mindset are dead works. However, **the mindset of the Spirit results in life and peace.** There is no surprise that in Colossians 3:2 Paul encourages believers *to set their minds on the things above, not the things on earth*. I like it! There is so much wisdom and encouragement in this statement. **So, what is the spiritual secret?** The secret of spiritual progress is not in *more religious work* or *more efforts* in the flesh trying to please God. **The secret of spiritual progress is in *yielding to the Holy Spirit* and *adopting the mind of Christ*,** as Paul writes in 1 Corinthians 2:16: "For WHO HAS KNOWN THE MIND OF THE LORD, THAT HE WILL INSTRUCT HIM? **But we have the mind of Christ.**" And having the attitude of Christ as instructed in

Victorious

"Have this attitude in yourselves which was also in Christ Jesus." (Philippians 2:5).

Reflection Questions:

Please reflect upon the following questions, briefly elaborate, then share your thoughts with a friend or with your small group.

1. What did the Holy Spirit whisper to your heart through this chapter?

_____

_____

2. What new concepts did you learn from this chapter? Which idea are you committed to implementing in your life?

_____

_____

3. What is the *agony* that all believers identify with, without exception?

_____

_____

_____

4. What are your thoughts regarding the two mindsets: 1. *The mindset of the flesh*, and 2. *The mindset of the Spirit*?

_____

_____

_____

5. Please list the best aha moments you had while reading this chapter.

_____

_____

Endnotes:

47 „The force (F) of attraction between two masses is directly proportional to the product of their masses and inversely proportional to the square of the distance (R) between their centers. This is all multiplied by a universal constant (G) whose value was determined by Henry Cavendish in 1798 {[Big G] value is 6.74 x 10^{-11} m^3 (cubic meters) per Kg^{-2} (kilogram - second squared} in 1798. www.nasa.gov. Accessed on April 6, 2024. [F = G (M1 m2) / R^2]. https://imagine.gsfc.nasa.gov/features/yba/CygX1_mass/gravity/more.html.

48 "Isaac Newton: Who He Was, Why Apples Are Falling." www.nationalgeographic.org. Accessed on February 23, 2024. https://education.nationalgeographic.org/resource/isaac-newton-who-he-was-why-apples-are-falling/.

49 Valy Vaduva, *Călătoria transformării,* (Upper Room Fellowship Ministry, Livonia, MI, 2018), 139.

50 "Taking Flight: The 4 Laws of Aerodynamics Explained," published on April 1, 2023. www.panairflighttraining.com. Accessed on April 6, 2024. https://www.panairflighttraining.com/post/taking-flight-the-4-laws-of-aerodynamics-explained

51 *The Normal Christian Life,* 188.

52 Nee, 189, 190.

53 Ibid, 183.

-4-

The Law Empowers Sin

For the law of the Spirit of life in Christ Jesus has set you free from the law of sin and of death.
— Romans 8:2

Paul writes:

> O DEATH, WHERE IS YOUR VICTORY? O DEATH, WHERE IS YOUR STING?" The sting of death is sin, *and the power of sin is the law;* but thanks be to God, who gives us the victory through our Lord Jesus Christ. (1 Corinthians 15:55–57)

I want to ask you a simple question. Did the Law produce any transformation in people who observed it? Absolutely not. What (better yet, Who) does transforming work inside us? The Holy Spirit does. This is why Paul insists so much in his teaching to rely 100% on the grace of God. He encourages believers *to walk according to the Spirit*. This is the only pathway to spiritual victory and fruitfulness.

In Galatians 5:16–25, Paul contrasts the deeds of the flesh with the fruit of the Spirit. What a powerful contrast that is! The instruction is clear: "But I say, walk by the Spirit, and you will not carry out the desire of the flesh" (Galatians 5:16). Simply put, IF I want victory over the flesh I **must walk by the Spirit.** Most importantly, to understand that IF the Spirit leads me, I am not under the Law. (See Galatians 5:18). Wow! It sounds so simple on paper! **Why does it seem so hard in real life?**

The answer is because of the flesh. The flesh concept is complex, and some of its manifestations are often difficult to explain. The roots of the flesh run deeper than we can imagine, even down to the Garden of Eden. My point is that: "Flesh and flesh patterns come in various shapes and sizes. For a complete assessment of your particular flesh patterns, please consult the Appendix called "Flesh Patterns Self-Assessment Tool"[54] at the end of my book, *The Journey of Transformation.*

Humans Are Self Confident

Another aspect worth paying attention to is that, as human beings, we are conditioned from early childhood to prove to ourselves and others that **we can do it.** I observed this, over and over again (repeatedly), in my grandchildren. From learning to walk to helping me with the kitchen work. From coming down the slides to climbing the monkey bars. And everything in between.

Let me give you just a couple of examples. When I prepare pancakes for them in the morning, as soon as I bring out the ingredients, they come closer to the countertop and ask me: *"Bunu, may I see what you are doing?"* I bring a chair closer so they can watch the process. Then they ask: *"Bunu, can I do it? Can I mix the eggs and the pancake powder?"* Of course, I let them sit on the countertop, give them the whisk, and let them mix it. They are so happy! *"Bunu, do you see? I made the pancake stuff."* I praise them for all their small achievements.

When I take them to the nearby playground, some are happy and enjoy using the slides. But some of them climb the monkey bars. From up there, they shout: *"Bunu, watch me. I can climb the monkey bars."* I tell them I'm proud of them. And the examples can go on and on. They smile, laugh, and feel very good that the person who loves them notices them, affirms their successes, and praises them!

The main point is that we all grew up with the internal drive to achieve, please, and to be noticed and affirmed by our parents, grandparents, teachers, professors, youth leaders, pastors, managers, and so on. All of that is part of the growth process as human beings. In essence, the main characteristic of the flesh is pride. Pride is Lucifer's "invention." (Look up in Isaiah 14:13, 14, the five statements *"I will…"* Lucifer said.) Using his tactics, the *serpent of old* deceived Eve, and then Adam decided to act independently of God. Adam died, and all of us in him (in his DNA.) After that, all human beings learned to operate independently of God. Since childhood, we have wanted to be in charge; we don't want anybody else to call the shots. Toddlers will respond "no" approximately 400 times. They do not want to comply. They don't need someone else's help. And so, life goes on.

Live a Cruciform Life

But at some point, in life, we meet Jesus, or better yet, Jesus meets us. We give our life to Him and do our best *to walk, come down the slides, and even climb the monkey bars of faith.* Christians around us praise our small achievements. That makes us feel good inside. But after a while, Jesus calls us to become His disciples.[6] The Lord wants us to *deny ourselves, take up our cross daily and follow Him.* (See Luke 9:23). At the beginning, we are happy, but after a while, we notice that something inside us does not want to submit to His leadership fully. **That resistance comes mainly from our flesh.** Until and unless we are convinced that *"nothing good dwells in me (us), that is, in my flesh"* (Romans 7:18a), we are not ready to accept the work of the *cross "in the removal of the body of the flesh by the circumcision of Christ"* (Colossians 2:11b).

I'm sure you have heard the expression coined by Benjamin Franklin: "You can do anything you set your mind to." How many times have we heard that statement growing up? Hundreds of times, maybe thousands. With that mindset, many believers say: *"I can do that for God."* Being blinded by this way of thinking, we tend to keep striving to produce the fruit of the Spirit instead of submitting our entire being under the authority of the Holy Spirit. **He is the only option we have for the inside-out transformation.** The evidence of the deeper inner transformation is the fruit of the Sprit springing forth effortlessly in our lives. In essence, there is only one

---

[6] I wrote an entire book on discipleship titled *The Great Commission: A Closer Look at Why Discipleship Cannot Be Ignored.* If you are interested in learning more about what it means to be a disciple of Christ feel free to get the book by clicking into this link: https://amzn.to/41OsRe1.

fruit—**agape love**. From it bloom the other characteristics of love: *joy, peace, patience, kindness, goodness, faithfulness, gentleness, and self-control.* (See Galatians 5:22–23).

To drive his point home, Paul writes:

> Now those who belong to Christ Jesus have crucified the flesh with its passions and desires. **If we live by the Spirit, let us also walk by the Spirit.** (Galatians 5:24–25)

In other words, if our source for salvation is the Spirit of God (cf. John 3:3,6, 2 Corinthians 5:17), **let's subject ourselves to His supernatural leading by walking by the Spirit.** Moreover, Paul writes: "For all who are being led by the Spirit of God, these are sons of God" (Romans 8:14). So, what are you waiting for? Go ahead and live according to God's guidelines!

1. Spiritual Comprehension

Know that you know that your *old man* was crucified with Christ. What you used to be in Adam is gone; you are dead to sin.

2. Spiritual Calculation

Reckon yourself dead to sin and alive to God. Based on the facts we demonstrated previously, stop allowing sin to call the shots in your life.

3. Spiritual Submission

Present yourself to God. Willingly and

decisively, yield your entire being (all members and all faculties) at God's disposal as weapons of righteousness.

4. Spiritual Guidance

Walk in the Spirit. Being in Christ means living under a more powerful principle: **the law of the Spirit of life.** Go ahead: live your life according to who you are in Him and *walk in the Spirit*.

Limited by time and space, I tried my best to uncover many fundamental meanings hidden in the Book of Romans. Truth be told, I just scratched the surface of what it means to live victoriously in Christ.

Let me end this chapter with the words of Paul from Galatians 5:24–25: "Now those who belong to Christ Jesus have crucified the flesh with its passions and desires. If we live by the Spirit, let us also walk by the Spirit."

I hope you sensed in your heart that these truths are fundamental for walking a more victorious Christian life.

Before placing my pen down, let me pray that our eyes will be wide open to receive these truths.

Prayer of Illumination

> *For this reason I too, having heard of the faith in the Lord Jesus which exists among you and your love for all the saints, do not cease giving thanks for you, while making mention of you in my prayers; that the God of our Lord Jesus Christ, the Father of glory, may give to you a spirit of wisdom and of revelation in the knowledge of Him. I pray that the eyes of your heart*

may be enlightened, so that you will know what is the hope of His calling, what are the riches of the glory of His inheritance in the saints, and what is the surpassing greatness of His power toward us who believe. These are in accordance with the working of the strength of His might which He brought about in Christ, when He raised Him from the dead and seated Him at His right hand in the heavenly places, far above all rule and authority and power and dominion, and every name that is named, not only in this age but also in the one to come. And He put all things in subjection under His feet, and gave Him as head over all things to the church, which is His body, the fullness of Him who fills all in all. (Ephesians 1:15–23).

May the Spirit enable you to incorporate these truths through faith and operate under the jurisdiction of grace. Finally, brethren, may Christ empower you all to know, reckon, present yourselves to God, and walk in the Spirit. In His name, I pray, amen. May God bless you, my beloved.

Reflection Questions:

Please reflect upon the following questions, briefly elaborate, then share your thoughts with a friend or with your small group.

1. What did the Holy Spirit whisper to your heart through this chapter?
   _____
   _____

2. What new concepts did you learn from this chapter? Which idea are you committed to implementing in your life?
   _____
   _____

3. What are thoughts about the fact that *"the Law gives power to sin"*?
   _____
   _____
   _____
   _____

4. What does it mean to *"live a cruciform life"*?
   _____
   _____
   _____

5. Please list the best aha moments you had while reading this chapter.
   _____
   _____

Endnotes:

[54] *The Journey of Transformation,* 142.

-5-

Lectio Divina
Practicing God's Presence

Let the words of my mouth and the meditation of my heart Be acceptable in Your sight, O LORD, my rock and my Redeemer.
— *Psalm 19:14.*

Reality Check: *We live in a very noisy world.* We are bombarded with gigabytes of information every day. "According to a report by the University of California–San Diego, the average American consumes about 34 gigabytes of data and information every day. That was estimated to be the equivalent of 100,000 words heard or read every day."[55] It is like reading the entire The Hobbit (95,356 words) by J.R.R. Tolkien in one day. That is a lot of information. Overwhelming, isn't it?

The world is in a severe mental health crisis

According to CNN: "Nine out of 10 adults said they

believed that there's a mental health crisis in the US today."⁵⁶ The National Institute of Mental Health stated that over 50 million adults in America are experiencing a mental illness. As I wrote in my book Grace Rediscovered:

> The super-CPU of humankind—the human brain was not designed to be inundated from all angles with news about the coronavirus, politics, economics, and a grim future. All these things lead to hopelessness, depression, anxiety, and all kinds of phobias. No wonder many "CPUs" are getting closer to the brink of despair.⁵⁷

Moreover: "According to the World Health Organization, around 450 million people currently struggle with mental illness, making it the leading cause of disability worldwide."⁵⁸

The reality is that mental health issues, such as generalized anxiety disorder (GAD), panic disorder, phobias, social anxiety disorder, obsessive-compulsive disorder (OCD), and even post-traumatic stress disorder (PTSD) are experienced by Christians.

According to Lifeway Research, a renowned and respected source for insights on pastoral leadership, church ministry, and the beliefs and faith practices of Americans: "23 percent of pastors acknowledge they have personally struggled with a mental illness, and 49 percent of pastors say they rarely or never speak to their congregation about mental illness."⁵⁹

Does the Bible have a say in this? Yes. The Lord Jesus stated His ministry platform very clearly.

Dr. Luke writes:

> The Spirit of the Lord is upon me, because he has anointed me to preach good news to the poor. He has sent me to proclaim release to the captives and recovering of sight to the blind, to set free those who are oppressed, to proclaim the favorable year of the Lord. (Luke 4:18–19).

Unfortunately, the stigma attached to mental illness persists in many Christian churches. Sadly, only 51 percent of pastors are equipped and willing to preach and promote professional assessments and treatment to their flock. As a result, many Christians suffer in silence instead of getting the help they deserve.

The good news is that even though the church silently rejects them, Jesus does not turn His back on those stigmatized believers; He loves them and has a solution for them.

Too much screen time is harmful

According to the Mayo Clinic, too much screen time can be linked to obesity, irregular sleep, behavioral problems, impaired academic performance, violence, and so on, especially in younger kids. In the article "Brain health consequences of digital technology use," published in Dialogues in Clinical Neuroscience, was reported:

> Potential harmful effects of extensive screen time and technology use include heightened attention-deficit symptoms, impaired emotional and social intelligence, technology addiction, social isolation, impaired brain development, and disrupted sleep ... Multiple studies have drawn a link between

computer use or extensive screen time (e.g., watching television, playing videogames) and symptoms of attention-deficit hyperactivity disorder (ADHD). A 2014 meta-analysis indicated a correlation between media use and attention problems.[60]

How should Christ's disciples live in today's culture?

The answer is simple: **practicing spiritual disciplines under God's grace.** Even though it sounds simple, this could be complicated for many believers. As I wrote in *The Great Commission*:

> An authentic disciple has learned and practices spiritual disciplines. Disciple and discipline come from the same Latin root word—*discipulus*. A disciple of Christ is a disciplined person.[61]

Dr. Anderson writes: "Discipleship requires mental discipline. People who will not assume responsibility for their thoughts cannot be discipled."[62]

Lectio Divina

One of the disciplines that can help Jesus' followers tremendously during this chaotic time is *Lectio Divina*. It is the discipline of reading the Scriptures in a posture of meditation. It requires us to read a passage of the Word of God *slowly* and *prayerfully*. I underlined slowly and prayerfully. This practice is one of the best ways to deepen your intimacy with Christ.

Lectio Divina is an ancient monastic practice used by many believers today. The main objective of this discipline is not the accumulation of mere intellectual knowledge; it seeks a deeper spiritual understanding of Scripture by the power of the Holy Spirit. The Bible is not just a collection of books divided into the Old Testament and the New Testament. The Bible is the Word of God, which is: "living and active and sharper than any two-edged sword, and piercing as far as the division of soul and spirit, of both joints and marrow and able to judge the thoughts and intentions of the heart" (Hebrews 4:12). So, when we open the Bible God opens His mouth and speaks to us. Are you listening? Do you discern the small voice of the Holy Spirit? When was the last time you clearly discerned God's voice emanating from Scripture? If that was a long time ago, then I highly encourage you to incorporate Lectio Divina into your discipleship walk.

Lectio Divina (Latin: divine reading) was developed by Benedict of Nursia in the 6th century. This practice has four steps: *1. reading, 2. meditation, 3. prayer,* and *4. contemplation.*

Guidelines

For the next 30 days set your heart and mind on God's grace, Christ's loving-kindness, and Holy Spirit's power to transform you into Christ's likeness.

- *Choose a passage.* for example, Psalms 1:1-3, 9:9-10, 16:7-8, 23:1-4, 27:1,5,14, 30:1-2, 34:17-18, 51:10-12, 62:1-2, 91:14-16, 119:1-5, or 139:1-6.
- *Find a quiet place.* The fewer distractions

there are, the more you can concentrate on *Lectio Divina*. Allocate enough time, maybe twenty or thirty minutes, for reading, meditation, prayer, and contemplation.
- Time. Choose the best time in the day that suits you well for practicing Lectio Divina (divine reading and meditation.)

Some people prefer to practice this in the morning when their minds are rested and quiet. Others may like to do it at night when no other items are left on the "to-do" list. Still, other individuals may choose to practice this discipline during their lunch break. Whatever works best for you is okay. Just try to establish a rhythm that suits you. Approach each time with great expectation to hear God's voice in your heart.

Step One—*Reading*

Read the passage slowly and meditatively. Consider the verses you are reading delicious food for your inner being. Do not rush; take your time. Listen intently to the words. Do not hurry to understand it intellectually; acknowledge God's presence in the process. "Be still, and know (recognize and understand) that I am God" (Psalm 46:10a AMP). Wait on the Lord the Spirit to bring a personalized word (rhema) to your heart.

Step Two—*Meditation*

According to the Merriam-Webster Dictionary, meditation means: *"to focus one's thoughts on, reflect on or ponder over."*[63] Christian meditation is totally different than

Eastern meditation. In Eastern meditation, the focus is on emptying one's mind, attempting to connect and unify with the impersonal Cosmic Mind with the goal of perfecting oneself. In Christian meditation, the believer focuses on filling his mind with God's Word and concentrates on obedience to the Lord with the goal of being transformed inside out by the Holy Spirit.

I like the way the famous theologian J.I. Packer explains it:

> Meditation is the activity of calling to mind, and thinking over, and dwelling on, and applying to oneself, the various things that one knows about the works and ways and purposes and promises of God... It is an activity of holy thought, consciously performed in the presence of God, under the eye of God, by the help of God, as a means of communion with God.[64]

Therefore, Biblical meditation is like chewing food over and over again till all the nutrients are extracted and become nourishment for the body. So, after you read the passage, you start repeating short phrases or even words, musing over them, thinking them over, paying attention to the feeling they generate, and inviting the living Word to renew your mind. In other words, Christian meditation is a form of personal devotion during which we engage with the Lord, and with the help of the Holy Spirit, we get to know Him better, experience His love, and develop a deeper intimacy with God. To explore a different way to increase your intimacy with Christ, I encourage you to study Chapter 12, "The Power of Intimacy with Jesus," from my book *Fullness of Christ*.[7]

I advise you to avoid all forms of Eastern meditation, New Age, Transcendental Meditation, and other forms of non-biblical meditation. But when it comes to Christian meditation, we should fully embrace this practice which leads to growing in the grace and knowledge of our Lord resulting in spiritual transformation into Christlikeness.

Step Three—*Prayer*

Pray, based on the passage you read, phrase by phrase, or verse by verse. Don't rush. Let the words echo into your heart. Respond to God after each phrase.

Step Four—*Contemplation*

Be still. Converse with the Holy Spirit inside your heart. Ask Him to bring to your conscious mind anything He wants you to pay close attention to. Do not rush the process. Silently wait on God. Pay close attention. Is there an image, a place, or a phrase that the Spirit is bringing to your attention? Contemplate on the aspects God is presenting to you. Focus on His love, grace, and faithfulness. In the end, thank God and praise Him for His presence.

---

[7] Click on the link to get the book: https://amzn.to/3mTcDBp.

Reflection Questions:

Please reflect upon the following questions, briefly elaborate, then share your thoughts with a friend or with your small group.

1. What did the Holy Spirit whisper to your heart through this chapter?

_____

_____

2. What new concepts did you learn from this chapter? Which idea are you committed to implementing in your life?

_____

_____

3. What are thoughts about the fact that "*49 percent of pastors say they rarely or never speak to their congregation about mental illness*"?

_____

_____

4. What do you think about *Lectio Divina*"? Do you think that it can assist you in practicing the presence of God in your life?

_____

_____

_____

5. Please list the best aha moments you had while reading this chapter.

_____

_____

Endnotes:

[55] "How Much Information Does the Human Brain Learn Every Day?" Published on Jun 1, 2022. https://medium.com/@askwonder/how-much-information-does-the-human-brain-learn-every-day-92deaad459a6

[56] Deidre McPhillips, "90% of US adults say the United States is experiencing a mental health crisis," CNN/KFF poll findsCNN, updated on October 5, 2022. Accessed on July 28, 2023. https://www.cnn.com/2022/10/05/health/cnn-kff-mental-health-poll-wellness/index.html.

[57] Valy Vaduva, *Grace Rediscovered,* (Livonia, MI, Upper Room Fellowship Ministry, 2023), 95.

[58] "The Mental Health Crisis Is Real." www.camh.ca. Accessed on July 28, 2023. https://bit.ly/47dy7LB.

[59] "13 Stats on Mental Health and the Church," published on www.research.lifeway.com on May 1, 2018. Accessed on May 13, 2024. https://research.lifeway.com/2018/05/01/13-stats-on-mental-health-and-the-church/.

[60] Multiple MD and PhD authors, "Brain health consequences of digital technology use," Published in Dialogues in Clinical Neuroscience, on June 22, 2020. Accessed on July 25, 2023. https://www.ncbi.nlm.nih.gov/pmc/articles/PMC7366948/.

[61] Valy Vaduva, The Great Commission, (Livonia, MI, Upper Room Fellowship Ministry, 2020), 90.

[62] Neil T. Anderson, Victory over the Darkness, (Ventura, CA: Regal Books, 2000), 222.

[63] Meditate. www.merriam-webster.com. Accessed on July 27, 2023. https://www.merriam-webster.com/dictionary/meditate.

[64] J.I. Packer, *Knowing God,* (Downers Grove, IL, InterVarsity, 1973), 23.

Addendum A
Supremacy of Christ

We proclaim Him, admonishing every man and teaching every man with all wisdom, so that we may present every man complete in Christ.
— Colossians 1:28.

Therefore, if you have been raised up with Christ, keep seeking the things above, where Christ is, seated at the right hand of God.
— Colossians 3:1

In AD 60–61, Paul, while under house arrest in Rome, wrote the letter to the church in Colossae. Along with Ephesians, Philippians, and Philemon, it is part of the "Prison Letters." Even though he addressed these letters to the first-century Christian audience, speaking to their specific needs, the messages in each Prison Letter are still very influential and insightful to the Church in the twenty-first century.

According to BiblePlaces.Com:

> Colossae was located 120 miles (193 km) east of Ephesus in the Lycus River Valley in ancient

Phrygia, part of the Roman territory of Asia Minor. It was one of a triad of cities in the area (the other two being Laodicea and Hierapolis), resting at the foot of Mount Cadmus. Its biblical significance lies in the fact that the book of Colossians was addressed to the church here (Col 1:2) and that Philemon lived in this city.[65]

According to respected theologians, Paul did not plant the church in Colossae, but Epaphras established it. While visiting Paul, who was in prison in Rome, Epaphras shared some significant concerns about the erroneous teachings that infiltrated his church. This is the background story of the Epistle to the Colossians in broad strokes.

Among the erroneous teachings, the most dangerous heresies are:

1. *Depreciation of Christ* (cf. Colossians 1:15–20; 2:2–3,9)
2. *Asceticism* (cf. Colossians 2:21; cf. 2:23)
3. *Reliance on tradition and ceremonialism for sanctification* (cf. Colossians 2:11, 3:11)

After being informed about these significant errors, Paul felt responsible for correcting them one by one.

Error nr. 1—*Depreciation of Christ*

To correct this error, Paul underlines that the Lord Jesus Christ:

1. Reflects the image of God the Father (Colossian 1:15).

2. Is preeminent over all creation. By Christ, all things in the entire universe were created both *"visible and invisible"* (Colossians 1:16a).
3. Has total authority over absolutely everything, including *"thrones or dominions or rulers or authorities"* (Colossians 1:16b).
4. Holds *"all things together"* in the entire universe (Colossians 1:17).
5. Has supreme authority over the church; He is the *"head of the church"* (Colossians 1:18a).
6. Has absolute superiority since He has the *"first place in everything"* (Colossians 1:18b).
7. Is the *Redeemer* (Colossians 1:13, 14), and the *Reconciler* of humankind to the Father (Colossians 1:20–22).

All of these and much more are true simply because the will of God the Father was, is, and will always be: *"for all the fullness to dwell in Him"* (Colossians 1:19b). **This should settle any disputes and misunderstandings regarding the supremacy of Christ.**

Prayer for the Colossians

I love the way Paul prays for the Colossian believers:

> For this reason also, since the day we heard *of it,* we have not ceased to pray for you and to ask that you may be filled with the knowledge of His will in all spiritual wisdom and understanding, so that you will walk in a manner worthy of the Lord, to please *Him* in all respects, bearing fruit in every good

work and increasing in the knowledge of God; strengthened with all power, according to His glorious might, for the attaining of all steadfastness and patience; joyously giving thanks to the Father, who has qualified us to share in the inheritance of the saints in Light. (Colossians 1:9–12)

Without too much elaboration, here are a few key points emanating from his prayer:

1. Spiritual Knowledge—*you may be filled with the knowledge of His will.*[8]
2. Spiritual Walk—*you will walk in a manner worthy of the Lord to please Him in all respects.*
3. Spiritual Fruitfulness—*bearing fruit in every good work.*
4. Spiritual Strength—*strengthened with all power, according to His glorious might.*
5. Spiritual Steadfastness—*for the attaining of all steadfastness and patience.*

Oh, we need spiritual mentors like Paul in today's church! We desperately need mature and loving Christians to pour their wisdom and experience into our lives. We must submit ourselves as disciples, at least for a while, to mentors who have a deep, intimate knowledge of Christ and His Word through the power and inspiration of the Holy Spirit.

---

[8] For a deeper understanding of the "Spiritual Knowledge" I highly recommend you read the section titled "The Map of Spiritual Transformation" from my book *The Journey of Transformation: Becoming Like Christ Through Spiritual Metamorphosis*. Click on the link to buy the book: https://bit.ly/41HPFfp.

On the other hand, we need to pray for the local churches to promote discipleship, which leads to spiritual growth. Listen to Paul's words: "that their hearts may be encouraged, having been knit together in love, and attaining to all the wealth that comes from the full assurance of understanding, resulting in a *true knowledge of God's mystery, that is, Christ Himself*" (Colossians 2:2).

Having laid his spiritual platform by prayer, Paul expands and builds on each of these spiritual dimensions throughout his epistle. We should take time to investigate each spiritual aspect in detail and extract all the *golden nuggets* for our spiritual walk.

Without too much elaboration, here are my findings:

1. Spiritual Knowledge

First, Paul prayed that these believers "[that they] may be filled with the *knowledge* of His will in all spiritual wisdom and *understanding"* Colossians 1:9). In other words, Paul acknowledges that to be filled with the knowledge of His will, we, believers, need all the spiritual wisdom and understanding we can get from above. We need the Holy Spirit working in us and transforming our hearts and minds into Christ's likeness. This kind of knowledge and understanding is not mere human but **deep spiritual knowledge.**

In other letters, Paul explains: "But a natural man does not accept the things of the Spirit of God, for they are foolishness to him; and he cannot understand them, because they are spiritually appraised" (1 Corinthians 2:14). **Obviously, the natural mind cannot comprehend the things of God.** Only a mind that the Spirit has touched can start seeing them. That is why

God's illumination is so important when reading the Scriptures.

Furthermore, Paul explains: "For to us God revealed them through the Spirit; for the Spirit searches all things, even the depths of God" (1 Corinthians 2:10). So, when we open *The Book*, before reading from it, we should pray, asking God to reveal to us the things of Christ by the Holy Spirit and guide us in all truth.

Jesus tells us: "But when He, the Spirit of truth, comes, He will guide you into all the truth; for He will not speak on His own initiative, but whatever He hears, He will speak; and He will disclose to you what is to come" (John 16:13). Without the Spirit's leading and guiding, we may read and understand the *words* on the pages of the Bible, but only with the Spirit's assistance may we **know Christ** and **His will**.

Jesus continues: "He will glorify Me, for He will take of Mine and **will disclose it to you**" (John 16:14). Wow! Did you see that? The Holy Spirit is the One Who *takes* of Christ and *reveals* Him to us. Marvelous! Why is this so wonderful? In the end, what matters is *"Christ in you, the hope of glory"* (Colossians 1:27(b)). Do you see it? Only by having the Scriptures *revealed, explained,* and *disclosed* to us by the Holy Spirit may we *"be filled with the knowledge of His will"* (Colossians 1:9).

Let's pray:

> O, heavenly Father, give us *all spiritual wisdom and understanding* (Colossians 1:9) to comprehend with all the saints (Ephesians 3:18) what it means to be *in Christ* and the significance of *Christ in us*, the hope of glory. We desire to know *the mystery which has been hidden from the past ages and generations*

(Colossians 1:26). Not only this, but our deep desire is for You to continue to manifest this mystery to Your saints and believers in the twenty-first century as You did it in the first century. We ask and pray that You continue filling us up with *all the fullness of God* (Ephesians 3:19). In Jesus' name, we pray, amen.

We live in a culture that pushes us into busyness, leading to terrible stress. And for what? I like the new song by For King and Country, "What Are We Waiting For?" released a few months ago. Here are the lyrics:

What are we waiting for? (Waiting for, waiting for)
What are we waiting for? (Waiting for)
Oh-oh-oh-oh-oh
…
So, what are we waiting for?
What are we waiting for?
Why are we wasting all the time like someone's making more?
What are we praying for?
What are we saving for?
What if we could be the light that no one could ignore?
What are we waiting for?

We have earthly obligations and family responsibilities, but as C. S. Lewis stated in *Mere Christianity*: "If you read history, you will find that the Christians who did most for the present world were just those who thought most of the next."[66] So, what are we waiting for? What are we praying for? What are we saving for? Let these questions sink in. Let's not lose perspective of the primary meaning in life—**knowing Christ and making Him know.**

2. Spiritual Walk

This aspect deals with the practical part of Christianity—*living out our faith.* We cannot just talk the talk; we must apply Christ's teachings through the Holy Spirit daily. In other words—*we must walk the walk.*

Paul insists on this practical aspect of Christianity in all his epistles. Later, in Colossians, Paul writes: "Therefore as you have received Christ Jesus the Lord, so walk in Him" (Colossians 2:6). Hm! "Walk in Him." What does Paul mean by these words? Feel free to do your digging. Here are the golden nuggets I found during my study:

- *Walk in Him* means living our lives from our spiritual center—*Christ.*

Paul explains this secret in Colossians 2:12. **God made us alive with Christ.** In other words, everything Christ went through 2000 years ago—*crucifixion, death, burial, resurrection,* and *ascension*—is true for us, too.

Some may ask: *How is this possible?* I live in the twenty-first century. I am alive now. How in the world are you telling me that I was buried with Christ and then I was raised with Him? Very simple! Because God has put you and me in Christ. At salvation, God took us spiritually out of Adam and placed us spiritually into Christ. In other words, we participated literally in Christ's death, burial, resurrection, and ascension and are seated at the Father's right hand. It is part of the Gospel. **This is the whole message of salvation.**

This is what the Word of God teaches us. It is part of our faith. Let's reread this verse: *"Having been buried with Him in baptism, in which you were also raised up with Him through faith in the working of God, who raised Him from the dead"* (Colossians 2:12). Wonderful news!? Of course it is! We have a new identity. We are not just sinners saved by grace. We are saints seated with Christ at the right hand of the Father. Yes! You read it correctly. This is our new identity. Even though we are here on this earth and live in this present culture, spiritually speaking, God "seated us with Him in the heavenly places in Christ Jesus" (Ephesians 2:6b). I underlined it: this is our new identity.

- ### Walk in Him means living a crucified life

What do I mean by that? Living a crucified life[9] means having the flesh with its manifestations brought daily to the cross of Christ. Paul explains this concept in Galatians. He writes: "Now those who belong to Christ Jesus have crucified the flesh with its passions and desires" (Galatians 5:24). In other words, Christians, because of their genuine relationship with Christ, through the Holy Spirit, have real victory over their own flesh.

Paul writes:

> So then, brethren, we are under obligation, not to the flesh, to live according to the flesh – for if you are living according to the flesh, you must die; but if by the Spirit you are putting to death the deeds

---

[9] Author's Note: For a deeper understanding of the "crucified life" I highly recommend you read, at least the "Preface" from my book *Fullness of Christ: Expressing God's Nature and Character in and through you.* Click on the link to buy the book: https://amzn.to/3mTcDBp.

of the body, you will live. (Romans 8:12–13)

Living a crucified life does not necessarily refer to a set of **don'ts** and going over a list of **dos**. Oh, no! Living a crucified life is not a new religion. Paul warns the believers in Colossae about the danger of falling into another religion of **don'ts** and **dos**. He writes: "See to it that no one takes you captive through philosophy and empty deception, according to the tradition of men, according to the elementary principles of the world, rather than according to Christ" (Colossians 2:8).

It's too bad that many believers today recite the sinner's prayer and ask Jesus to come into their hearts. Then, <u>due to a lack of proper discipleship</u>, they try to walk the walk by keeping all sorts of rules and regulations without deepening their relationship with their Savoir. Living with a perpetual sense of duty and fear of punishment is not real living.

Paul drives it home with these words:

> Let no one keep defrauding you of your prize by delighting in *self-abasement* ..., inflated without cause by his fleshly mind, and <u>not holding fast to the Head</u>, from whom the entire body, being supplied and held together by the joints and ligaments, grows with a growth which is from God. (Colossians 2:18–19)

Did you hear Paul's words? The secret of spiritual growth is holding fast to the Head. Being in an organic relationship with the Head—Christ, is the only position *resulting in growth from God.*

Living out of an intimate relationship with Christ

based on love and reverence is the best life ever. It is the manifestation of Christ's life in and through our life. Yes, this is a mystery! The best way I know to describe this mystery is to recite what Paul teaches: "I have been crucified with Christ; and it is no longer I who live, but Christ lives in me; and the life which I now live in the flesh I live by faith in the Son of God, who loved me and gave Himself up for me" (Galatians 2:20).

- *Walk in Him* means walking by the Spirit

Paul writes: *"If we live by the Spirit, let us also walk by the Spirit"* (Galatians 5:24). This type of living is not a run. It is not seating either. It is walking in the Spirit. The Spirit moves, we move. The Spirit turns this way; we turn that way, too. It is a life lived in harmony with the Holy Spirit. He leads us; we follow Him. These, indeed, are the mature sons and daughters of God. Paul writes: "For all who are being led by the Spirit of God, these are sons of God" (Romans 8:14).

The sad part is that many Christians (due to a lack of proper discipleship leading to spiritual maturity) do not walk under the guidance of the Holy Spirit but according to their fleshly desires. This sad reality broke Paul's heart many times.

To the Philippians, he writes:

> For many **walk**, of whom I often told you, and now tell you even weeping, that they are **enemies of the cross of Christ**, whose end is destruction, whose god is their appetite, and whose glory is in their shame, who set their minds on earthly things. (Philippians 3:18–19)

Wow! Many Christians walk as enemies of the cross of Christ. Clearly, these people have their minds set on earthly things rather than on the things from above, as Paul admonishes believers to do in Colossians 3:2.

Moreover, walking by the Spirit means setting our minds on the things of the Spirit. Paul writes: "For those who are according to the flesh set their minds on the things of the flesh, but those who are according to the Spirit, the things of the Spirit" (Romans 8:5). This requires a continual renewal of the mind (see Romans 12:2, Ephesians 4:23).

In my book *Grace Rediscovered*, I wrote:

> In Paul's teaching, righteousness is a critical part of the believers' spiritual identity, and it must be at the foundation of any born-again believer. Only after this doctrine sinks in deeper, Christ's disciples are motivated and energized from the inside out by the Holy Spirit to "walk in newness of life", (Romans 6:4b), "walk by the Spirit" (Galatians 5:16a), "walk in love" (Ephesians 5:2a), "walk in a manner worthy of the Lord" (Colossians 1:10a), and "walk in a manner worthy of the God who calls you" (1 Thessalonians 2:12). From Paul's point of view, and I subscribe to it 100%, the Christian life is supernatural and cannot be lived based on human efforts. Only "Christ in you, (is) the hope of glory" (Colossians 1:27b). Paul writes: "If we live by the Spirit, let us also walk by the Spirit" (Galatians 5:25).[67]

Why not take some time to meditate on our spiritual center—Christ? Feel free to use *Lectio Divina*—literally

Victorious

divine reading (see Addendum A) and immerse yourself in the Scriptures very personally. Even though we live in a noisy and stressful world, it is up to us to walk in Him and live a crucified life. We should not lose focus on the fact that this world is not our permanent home; we are sojourners toward our permanent home—heaven. So, let's focus on the things above, not on the things of this earth (cf. Colossians 3:1–3). **Let's walk by the Spirit.**

Endnotes:

[65] Colossae, www.bibleplaces.com. Accessed on August 25, 2023. https://www.bibleplaces.com/colossae/.
[66] C. S. Lewis, *Mere Christianity*, (HarperCollins, New York, NY, 2001) 134.
[67] Valy Vaduva, *Grace Rediscovered: In Awe of God's Lovingkindness* (Upper Room Fellowship Ministry, Livonia, MI, 2023), 71,72. Click on the link to buy the book: https://amzn.to/3rc9gqW.

Addendum B
Christ Plus Nothing

> *If you have died with Christ to the elementary principles of the world, why, as if you were living in the world, do you submit yourself to decrees, such as, "Do not handle, do not taste, do not touch!"*
> — *Colossians 2:20–21*

Let's unpack things from Colossians 2:1–6. Paul continues to encourage the believers in Colossae to practice brotherly love so they could get to a level of assurance and understanding *"resulting in a true knowledge of God's mystery that is Christ himself"* (Colossians 2:2). The Lord Jesus has <u>all the wisdom</u> and <u>the knowledge</u> necessary for any believer and local church to grow and mature spiritually.

Error nr. 2—Asceticism

Growing in *"the grace and knowledge of our Lord and Savior Jesus Christ"* (2 Peter 3:18a) is the only way to error-proof our faith and shield ourselves from any "persuasive argument" employed by some people in the church to dilute the power *"of the gospel of the grace of God"* (Acts 20:24a).

Paul's statement is crystal clear: "Therefore as you have received Christ Jesus the Lord, so walk in Him" (Colossians 2:6). How have we believers received Christ? In other words, how have we been saved? We know this from Sunday School: "For by grace you have been saved through faith; and that not of yourselves, it is the gift of God" (Ephesians 2:8). Many of us already memorized this crucial verse. Therefore, walking in Him must be by grace through faith.

Furthermore, Paul gives believers the stages for growing strong in God's family. In Colossians 2:7, Paul states: "Having been firmly rooted (*past tense*) and now being built up in Him (*present continuous*) and established in your faith, (*future result*) just as you were instructed, and overflowing with gratitude (*the attitude of a mature believer*)."

In summary, the stages for growing strong in God's family are:

1. Firmly rooted
2. Built up in Christ
3. Established in faith

Reflecting on Colossians 2:7, I imagine a young and frail fruit tree recently planted in the garden. Before producing any fruits, it must be firmly rooted in the new ground. Then, it must *grow* and *mature* until it is fully established; **then it can bear fruit.**

This should be the story of any believer who reached a place of stability in faith through proper discipleship and mentorship, leading to spiritual fruitfulness. We must recognize all the stages in our spiritual journey and follow all of God's guidelines.

As a seasoned and wise teacher, Paul does not let the believers from Colosse guess what accurate theology looks like. He writes to them in concrete terms, the foundation of the Christian faith. Verses nine to fifteen are crucial and must be adequately understood.

Without too much elaboration, based on Colossians 2:11-12, let me mention some of Paul's important points:

- **Christ is fully God and fully man.** He is the exact representation of Deity[10] (Colossians 2:9, Hebrews 1:3).
- **Christ has complete authority,** *"and in Him, we have been made complete"* (Colossians 2:10).
- **Christ is the Spiritual Surgeon** who circumcised our hearts by removing the **old man** from our system (Colossians 2:11, Romans 6:6).
- **In Christ, we were both buried and raised to life.** Water baptism is not a Christian ritual; it communicates a profound spiritual reality. When we were immersed in the baptismal water—we were *"buried with Him"* (Colossians 2:12a). And when we rose out from the baptismal water—"we were also raised with Him through faith" (Colossians 2:12b).

After these aspects, Paul expands on the meaning of forgiveness and reconciliation (Colossians 2:13–15):

---

[10] Autor's Note: The concept "He is the exact representation of Deity" is fully explained in the section titled "Charakter" from my book *The Journey of Transformation*.

- Christ's resurrection is the proof that we are justified—*just-as-if-I'd*[11] never sinned (Romans 4:25). This means that on the Cross, Jesus paid in full the penalty of our sins, and through His powerful resurrection, He completely forgave *"us all our transgressions"* (Colossians 2:13).
- Christ canceled our debt certificate. The work of the cross[12] is more profound than many believers know. He completely removed all the decrees that were against us *"having nailed it to the cross"* (Colossians 2:14). In other words, Christ nailed the Law to the cross; *therefore, we are no longer under the Law, but under Grace* (Romans 6:14b).
- Christ *"disarmed the rulers and authorities"* (Colossians 2:15a) through the cross and resurrection. God *"rescued us from the domain of darkness and transferred us to the kingdom of His beloved Son"* (Colossians 1:13). This is mindboggling!

These truths are crucial for a thriving faith. Lacking experiential knowledge in this area leads to confusion and defeat. The Old Testament prophet states: "My people are destroyed for lack of knowledge" (Hosea 4:6a). Similarly, the New Covenant believers are in danger of remaining spiritually immature and easily influenced by false

---

[11] Author's Note: The term "justification" may intimidate some believers. I urge you to read the "Justification" section from my book *Grace Rediscovered*. It will make it easier to wrap your arms around this crucial theological term.

[12] Author's Note: The Church exists for only one reason—the CROSS. To understand the concept of the cross deeper, I encourage you to read the chapter titled "The Power of the Cross" from my book *Fullness of Christ*.

doctrines, such as *asceticism*.

According to Encyclopedia Britannica: "asceticism, (derives from Greek *askeō*: "to exercise," or "to train"), (and is) the practice of the denial of physical or psychological desires in order to attain a spiritual ideal or goal."[68]

Paul warns us: "These are matters which have, to be sure, *the appearance of wisdom* in self-made religion and *self-abasement* and *severe treatment of the body*, but are of no value against fleshly indulgence" (Colossians 2:23). Does God ask us anywhere in the New Testament to treat our physical body severely? Of course not. In other letters, such as 1 Corinthians 2:24–27, Paul uses the Olympics to illustrate how athletes prepare for the competition by exercising self-control to receive a *"perishable wreath."* How much more should Christians employ self-control to acquire *"an imperishable wreath"* (1 Corinthians 9:25)? However, when Paul says "self-control," he does not suggest or imply "self-abasement."[69] For example, one of the synonyms of "self-abasement" is "ignominy" and according to Merriam-Webster Dictionary, it means: "deep personal humiliation and disgrace."[70] Let's ask ourselves: "Does Christ want us to entertain a deep sense of shame? Of course not.

Error nr. 3—Reliance on tradition and ceremonialism for sanctification

Traditions significantly affect religious people, including Christians. In most cases, religion is transmitted down from generation to generation. Children learn about religious beliefs and practices from their parents. We are all influenced a lot or a little by the traditions we observe in our cultures. More often than not, people's beliefs and practices are shaped by those traditions.

Traditions in themselves are not bad. Traditions keep communities together and give people a sense of belonging. But when Christians mix traditions with faith and consider them part of their Christian living and spiritual growth, it becomes a huge problem. Paul raised the red flag: "See to it that no one takes you captive through philosophy and empty deception, according to the tradition of men, according to the elementary principles of the world, rather than according to Christ" (Colossians 2:8).

Observing certain holidays, new moons, keeping the Sabbath day, and similar practices were very important for the Jews during that time. The mixing of Christianity and practices of the Law was widespread during Paul's ministry.

In a particular instance, even Peter and Barnabas were caught in this trap and acted hypocritically. When they were among the Gentiles, they ate freely with them, but when Hebrew Christians from Jerusalem arrived, they left their seats and distanced themselves from the Gentile Christians (Galatians 2:11–12). Paul was present then and publicly confronted Peter: "If you, being a Jew, live like the Gentiles and not like the Jews, how is it that you compel the Gentiles to live like Jews?" (Galatians 2:14b). Auch!

To the believers in Colossae, Paul writes:

> Therefore, no one is to act as your judge in regard to food or drink or in respect to a festival or a new moon or a Sabbath day—things which are a mere shadow of what is to come; but the substance

belongs to Christ. (Colossians 2:16–17)

According to Paul, these aspects are just elementary principles of the world "but are of no value against fleshly indulgence" (Colossians 2:23b).

Great Dangers

As Christians, our spiritual identity is 100% linked to Christ. We died with Him, and we were raised with Him. Therefore, we do not have to submit ourselves, not even for a second, to man-made religious principles like these: *"Do not handle, do not taste, do not touch!"* (Colossians 2:21).

In my book *Grace Rediscovered*, I exposed these great dangers:

> *1. Mixing the Law with grace leads to legalism, which makes God's grace in vain.* "You have been severed from Christ, you who are seeking to be justified by law; you have fallen from grace. (Galatians 5:4).

> *2. Using God's grace as a license to sin leads to licentiousness and makes faith ineffective.* "What shall we say then? Are we to continue in sin so that grace may increase? May it never be! How shall we who died to sin still live in it?" (Romans 6:1, 2).[71]

In other words, since we are *"not under law but under grace"* (Romans 6:14b), we should be very careful not to mix grace with the law. This is dangerous because it weakens the influence of God's grace in our lives and stagnates our spiritual growth.

Let all of us be encouraged by Paul's words: "May the Lord direct your hearts into the love of God and into the steadfastness of Christ" (2 Thessalonians 3:5). Amen and amen.

Endnotes:

[68] Asceticism. www.britannica.com. Accessed on September 27, 2023. https://www.britannica.com/topic/asceticism.

[69] Explanatory Note: "Self-control" is not synonymous with "self-abasement." Synonyms for self-abasement are confusion, degradation, disgrace, and ignominy. (Self-abasement. www.thesaurus.com. Accessed on September 30, 2023. https://www.thesaurus.com/browse/self-abasement.".

[70] Ignominy: "deep personal humiliation and disgrace." www.merriam-webster.com. Accessed on September 30, 2023. https://www.merriam-webster.com/dictionary/ignominy.

[71] *Grace Rediscovered*, 60.

Addendum C
Hidden with Christ in God

For you have died and your life is hidden with Christ in God. When Christ, who is our life, is revealed, then you also will be revealed with Him in glory.
— *Colossians 3:3–4*

Let us look at Paul's superb teaching in Colossians 3. This chapter starts with the adverb *"therefore."* Remember that every time we read the Bible and stumble across "therefore," we should pause and ask ourselves: "What's the *"therefore,"* there for?" According to the Merriam-Webster Dictionary, the adverb "therefore" means "1. a. for that reason; consequently, b. because of that, c. on that ground."[72]

Paul writes:

> Therefore, if you have been raised up with Christ, keep seeking the things above, where Christ is, seated at the right hand of God. Set your mind on the things above, not on the things that are on earth. For you have died and your life is hidden with Christ in God. When Christ, who is our life,

is revealed, then you also will be revealed with Him in glory. (Colossians 3:1–4)

In other words, "on the ground" established by Paul in Colossians chapters 1 and 2, he urges believers to earnestly think, feel, and live according to their spiritual position— *"seated with Him [Christ] in the heavenly"* (Ephesians 2:6b). The expression "keep seeking" is present continuous tense, which means the current activity is carried consistently into the future. I like how Eugene Peterson renders it: *"Pursue the things over which Christ presides"* (Colossians 3:1–2 MSG).

In verse 2, Paul instructs: *"Set your mind on the things above."* This conveys the idea that the believer's mind has a spiritual dimension that must be intentionally directed toward the things above. A mentor from long ago explained it this way: *"Christians are called to set their minds on things above; otherwise, their minds, by default, remain set on things of this earth."*

In verse 3, Paul underlines why he is asking believers to be heavenly-minded: *"For you have died, and your life is hidden with Christ in God."* Since Christ is seated at the right hand of the Father and our real life is directly linked to Him, our thoughts, affections, and meditations should focus first and foremost on the Kingdom of God more than anything in this world.

In other words, our Christian living should be congruent with our spiritual position. This comes with an exceptional promise: *"When Christ is revealed, then you also will be revealed with Him in glory"* (Colossians 3:4). Powerful!

In the Sermon on the Mount, Jesus teaches: "But seek first His kingdom and His righteousness, and all these things will be added to you" (Matthew 6:33). So, as believers, we don't have to chase the things if this world; we should seek God's Kingdom, and the Fathers takes care of our needs.

If verses 1–4 from Colossians 3 are correctly understood and diligently applied, then the Christian living is meaningful and progresses toward *"completeness in Christ"* (Colossians 1:27b).

Verses 5–16 contain very practical instructions for daily living. Keep in mind that verse 5 begins with another "therefore." Paul writes:

> Therefore, consider the members of your earthly body as dead to immorality, impurity, passion, evil desire, and greed, which amounts to idolatry. For it is because of these things that the wrath of God will come upon the sons of disobedience, and in them you also once walked, when you were living in them. But now you also, put them all aside: anger, wrath, malice, slander, and abusive speech from your mouth. (Colossians 3:5–8)

Because of what Paul emphasized in verses 1–4, primarily because we have died and our life is directly linked with Christ, we should consider everything in the here and now from the finished work of Christ on the cross. Two thousand years ago, when Jesus died, we also died with Him. Because of our co-crucifixion[13] with Christ (Galatians 2:20), the members of our earthly body should be treated as dead to the influences of the world,

---

[13] The concept of co-crucifixion is largely explained in chapter 7 "The Greatest Exchange Ever" of my book *Fullness of Christ*. Click on the link to buy the book: https://amzn.to/3mTcDBp.

the flesh, and the devil, such as: *"immorality, impurity, passion, evil desire, and greed, which amounts to idolatry"* (Colossians 3:5). Our living style as believers should radically differ from our old life before we were born again.

Moreover, since our lives belong to Christ and the Holy Spirit indwells us, we have the authority to put aside *"anger, wrath, malice, slander, and abusive speech"* (Colossians 3:8). In other words, these negative characteristics should no longer dominate believers.

- *Anger:* an emotion characterized by antagonism toward someone or something you feel has deliberately done you wrong,[73] must be handled biblically considering Ephesians 4:26–27, then laid aside.
- *Wrath:* a strong feeling of hatred or resentment with a desire for vengeance, must be put aside.
- *Malice:* deliberate ill-will, or wickedness,[74] must be dealt with once and for all.
- *Slander* (diaballo, Latin scandalum), to calumniate: an accusation maliciously uttered, with the purpose or effect of damaging the reputation of another,[75] must be immediately laid aside.
- *Abusive speech:* any language that insults, demeans the dignity of an individual, is harsh, violent, profane, or derogatory, including profanity and racial, ethnic, or sexist slurs, must be done away with once and for all.[76]

None of these characteristics belong to a follower of

Christ. Yet, how many times have we acted in anger, harbored resentments towards a parent, spouse, or church leader, hurried with accusations towards someone without having enough evidence, or employed a harsh or intimidating tone of voice with coworkers and relatives?

The Bible states very clearly that if before we walked in these characteristics as *"son of disobedience"* (Colossians 3:6), now we should *"walk as children of Light"* (Ephesians 5:8b). If anything from the old life still lingers in our lives, we have some serious repentance to do because disobedience and darkness have nothing to do with a genuine believer.

Paul continues his train of thought in verses 9–11:

> Do not lie to one another, since you laid aside the old self with its evil practices, and have put on the new self who is being renewed to a true knowledge according to the image of the One who created him—a renewal in which there is no distinction between Greek and Jew, circumcised and uncircumcised, barbarian, Scythian, slave and freeman, but Christ is all, and in all. (Colossians 3:9–11)

Did you hear what Paul wrote? *Believers have laid aside the old self.* As I read verse 9, my mind went to Romans 6:6: "knowing this, that our old self was crucified with Him, in order that our body of sin might be done away with, so that we would no longer be slaves to sin."[14] Please underline *we would no longer be slaves to sin.* If spiritually

---

[14] For more in-depth understanding of this please revisit: "God's Guidelines for Successful Living." There we investigated in greater detail Paul's teaching in Romans 6:1–14.

speaking, we are no longer slaves to sin, why do we still tolerate sin in our lives? This does not make sense. Sinning is not compatible with Christianity.

Put off, and put on

A few years ago, my wife and I were in Mexico for a time of rest, relaxation, and spiritual recharging. A few days after our arrival, I was invited to preach at a Mexican Church near our resort. It was, for sure, a powerful experience! I wrote all the details of that experience in my book *The Journey of Transformation*.[15]

> Upon receiving the invitation, I just whispered a short prayer under my breath: "Lord, what would you like me to preach?" Immediately after, the phrase "Put On" from Ephesians resonated in my heart. I picked up the New Testament and looked for all the main verses where Paul exhorts us using this short phrase.[77]

Paul continues:

> So, as those who have been chosen of God, holy and beloved, put on a heart of compassion, kindness, humility, gentleness and patience; bearing with one another, and forgiving each other, whoever has a complaint against anyone; just as the Lord forgave you, so also should you. Beyond all these things put on love, which is the perfect bond of unity. (Colossians 3:12–14)

---

[15] Click on the link to buy *The Journey of Transformation*: https://bit.ly/41HPFfp.

Paul goes on connecting the earlier thoughts from verse 8: *"put them all aside"* and *"you laid aside the old self"* from verse 9, with the imperative "put on" in verses 10, 12 14. f you search the Bible app and type *"put on,"* you will find approximately eight imperatives: *"put on,"* two in Romans, three in Ephesians, and three in Colossians. I recorded the entire list of *"put off, and put on"* in *The Journey of Transformation*. In this book I wrote:

> I like to sleep in my pajamas, but I don't go to church in my pajamas. For example, on Sunday morning, I make a conscious decision to put off my pajamas and put on different clothes. My clothes don't just automatically fall on me; that would be nice. I decide what to wear and, piece by piece, I put on my particular outfit for the day.
> This is similar in the spiritual realm. When we are born again, in an instant, we become brand new beings (2 Corinthians 5:17). Our spirit is miraculously changed, but "stuff" from our "former manner of living" (Ephesians 4:22a), referred to as the "flesh," is still there. The human soul of a saved person does not change instantly; it must enter a process of **progressive sanctification**. This is not automatic. We must decide to surrender our bodies (Romans 12:1) and invite the Holy Spirit to transform our souls.[78]

- Believers who used to have a bad temper before they got saved will not become patient people overnight; *they must put on patience.*
- Individuals who were vengeful before becoming Christians will not forgive instantly when

wronged; *they must put on a heart of compassion.*
Let's place side by side what Paul wrote in verses 8 and 12:

Colossians 3:8	Colossians 3:12
anger	heart of compassion
wrath	kindness
malice	humility
slander	gentleness
abusive speech	patience

- Christians who were gossipers before they were saved will tend to bad mouth other people. They don't get immune to this behavior just because they go to church; *they must put on humility.*
- People who were verbally abused growing up have a higher tendency to be verbally abusers later in life, *they must put on gentleness.* They will not be gentle just because they are part of a Small Group and participate in Bible Studies; *they must be intentional about putting on gentleness.*

This is what I mean by progressive sanctification.

Furthermore:

Let the peace of Christ rule in your hearts, to which indeed you were called in one body; and be thankful. Let the word of Christ richly dwell within you, with all wisdom teaching and admonishing one another with psalms and hymns and spiritual songs, singing with thankfulness in your hearts to God. Whatever you do in word or deed, do all in the name of the Lord Jesus, giving thanks through Him to God the Father. (Colossians 3:15–17)

What is Paul saying in these verses? What does *"Let the peace of Christ rule in your hearts"* mean? The word "rule" used here corresponds to Greek Strong # 1018, "βραβεύω," transliterated *"brabeuó,"* and means "to act as umpire." Colossians 3:15 is the only place in the New Testament where this specific word is used! The word is mainly used in sports and means *"to act as arbiter in the games"* to arbitrate over the competition. In other words, *"to decide as an umpire"* means "to make the call in a conflict between contending forces."[79]

Therefore, Paul says: *"Allow the peace of Christ arbitrate over your heart; let God's supernatural peace make the final call when there is inner or outer conflict. Let the Holy Spirit settle things the way He wants."*

As I wrote these things my thought went to Philippians 4:6—7:

> Be anxious for nothing, but in everything by prayer and supplication with thanksgiving let your requests be made known to God. And the peace of God, which surpasses all comprehension, will guard your hearts and your minds in Christ Jesus.

Did you see this idea again? *"The peace of God will guard your hearts and minds in Christ Jesus."* Incredible! What a powerful treatment against anxiety. When we have an anxiety attack, instead of taking Prozac, Lexapro, Celexa, Paxil, or Zoloft, we kneel and pray; ask God for His provisions in that particular situation, thank Him for everything, and boom—*God's powerful peace safeguards our hearts and minds.* Is that easy? I'm not against medication. Every individual situation is deferent. Seeking professional Mental Health isn't bad. Christian and Pastoral counseling helps tremendously, but nothing works as the power of the Holy Spirit.

By combining the thoughts, we discussed, Colossians 3:15 could sound like:

- *Let the peace of God be the umpire in your life and actions,* or:
- *Let the peace of God call the shots in your life,* or:
- *Let the peace of God act as a referee in your emotions and decisions.*

In verse 16, Paul tells us: *"Let the word of Christ richly dwell within you."* What does he mean by this exhortation? Paul is saying that the Logos of Christ must be resident in us. The word *"richly"* communicates abundance. This means that the Logos occupies all the rooms of our hearts, not just a tiny closet somewhere. I believe that Colossians 3:16 communicates the concept of having God's Word in abundance in our minds, so IT influences the entire spectrum of our existence. The verse continues: [Let the word of Christ richly dwell within you] "with all wisdom teaching and admonishing one another with psalms and hymns and spiritual songs."

As I wrote these ideas my thoughts went to 2 Timothy 3:16–17:

All Scripture is inspired by God and profitable for teaching, for reproof, for correction, for training in righteousness; so that the man of God may be adequate, equipped for every good work.

Knowing that the entire Bible from Genesis to Revelation is "God-breathed"—given by His inspiration (2 Timothy 3:16 AMP), should motivate us to have it in abundance in our hearts. What good would it do for us if the wisdom it contains is just inside the Bible but not inside our hearts? Jesus Himself states that: "Man shall not live and be upheld and sustained by bread alone, but by every word that comes forth from the mouth of God" (Matthew 4:4 AMP).

Paul concludes this section of his teaching with this axiom or principle: "Whatever you do in word or deed, do all in the name of the Lord Jesus, giving thanks through Him to God the Father" (Colossians 3:17). This means everything in the life of a born-again believer should be done to please the Lord Jesus, and with an attitude of thanksgiving. Wow! That is a high bar to live by. I agree, but being led by the Spirit and following God's guidelines we can live successful lives.

Victorious

Endnotes:

[72] Therefore. www.merriam-webster.com. Accessed on October 27, 2023. https://www.merriam-webster.com/dictionary/therefore.
[73] Anger. www.apa.org. Accessed on October 27, 2023. https://www.apa.org/topics/anger.
[74] Malice. www.biblestudytools.com. Accessed on October 27, 2023. https://bit.ly/47czJVn..
[75] Slander. www.biblestudytools.com. Accessed on October 27, 2023. https://www.biblestudytools.com/dictionary/slander/.
[76] Abusive language. www.lawinsider.com. Accessed on October 27, 2023. https://bit.ly/3MjdBjU.
[77] Valy Vaduva, *The Journey of Transformation: Becoming Like Christ Through Spiritual Metamorphosis*, (Upper Room Fellowship Ministry, Livonia, MI, 2021), 175.
[78] *The Journey of Transformation*, 177.
[79] Brabeuó, Strong Greek # 1018. Biblehub.com. Accessed on November 3, 2023. https://biblehub.com/greek/1018.htm.

Upper Room Fellowship Ministry

In 1996, in response to God's calling and with the guidance of the Holy Spirit, Upper Room Fellowship Ministry (URFM) was formed to serve the body of Christ. It is a non-profit and non-denominational Christian organization.

UPPER ROOM
FELLOWSHIP MINISTRY

Vision
Fully alive through mind renewal and spiritual transformation for God's glory.

Mission

We desire to assist believers in experiencing healing for the wounded heart, restoration for the soul, and spiritual growth in Christ. Our prayer and deep desire are that you experience Jesus Christ as your very source of life through the Holy Spirit.

Through individual or small group meetings and retreats, our ministry is committed to creating an environment where healing, restoration, and spiritual freedom can be experienced. Under the guidance of the Holy Spirit, URFM is making disciples and equipping them for the Kingdom of God. This organization ministers to the spiritual growth of all believers.

The goal is that every member of Christ's Body would attain the **Ultimate Intention**—*the fullness of Christ.*

Most Christians have been taught that Jesus Christ died for their sins. Some embraced Christ as their Lord. Only a few have been taught the truth that they died with Him and experienced Christ as their Life. Consequently, even fewer find victory in their lives. Although they have been set free from their sins, they have not been set free from themselves.

Our desire and fervent prayer for all of Jesus' disciples are that they all will become everything that God intends for them to become, in other words—the fullness of Christ.

About the author

Valy Vaduva was born in Romania, a beautiful country in Eastern Europe. He became a follower of Jesus at sixteen and started preaching the Gospel at seventeen. He loves the Bible and takes the Great Commission very seriously. Valy is passionate about spiritual growth. His greatest desire is to see believers grow up in all aspects in Jesus, be transformed by the Holy Spirit, and reach the fullness of Christ. Therefore, he loves working with believers who desire to grow in the grace and knowledge of Christ.

Valy is an ordained minister and the co-founder and president of the Upper Room Fellowship Ministry (URFM).

He earned his Master of Arts in Spiritual Formation and Leadership from Spring Arbor University.

As a certified Spiritual Life Coach, Valy offers personalized spiritual formation sessions in person and online. Valy and his wife, Elena, have four married children and ten grandchildren. They live in Michigan, USA.

www.ingramcontent.com/pod-product-compliance
Lightning Source LLC
Chambersburg PA
CBHW060331050426
42449CB00011B/2719